DATE DUE

James H. Humphrey

Childhood Stress
in Contemporary Society

Pre-publication
REVIEWS,
COMMENTARIES,
EVALUATIONS . . .

"This book is of inestimable value to parents, teachers, counselors, and others who deal with children because it explains in detail why stress can be so different for kids. It's interesting to note how rapidly daily hassles change from one age group to the next. This is useful information because children may not always tell you about what's really bothering them.

In addition to explaining the sources of stress and how to avoid them, this book also provides a thorough discussion of stress reduction techniques that have been found to be effective in children, including meditation, progressive muscular relaxation, and biofeedback. The importance of proper diet, regular exercise, and adequate sleep is emphasized as well as the powerful stress-buffering effects of strong social support."

Paul J. Rosch, MD, FACP
President, The American Institute of Stress;
Clinical Professor of Medicine
and Psychiatry,
New York Medical College

More pre-publication
REVIEWS, COMMENTARIES, EVALUATIONS . . .

"In modern-day society, children experience a great deal of stress. Who better to write a book to guide adults in understanding and helping children manage that stress than Dr. James Humphrey? Dr. Humphrey is a prolific author who has specialized in stress in children. He has even collaborated with Hans Selye on research in this area. His professional contributions have been recognized by his peers as evidenced by his being selected for several awards and honors. In *Childhood Stress in Contemporary Society*, Dr. Humphrey provides insight into the conception of stress and stressors, and relates that to stress encountered by children. He then proceeds to present strategies that adults can employ to provide children with the resources they need to transverse their stressful world. The comprehensive nature of this book is evident when considering chapters titled "Childhood Emotions"; "Stress and the Child with an Affliction"; and "Nutrition, Diet, and Stress." Dr. Humphrey ends with several chapters describing relaxation techniques (progressive relaxation, meditation, and biofeedback) that have been successful as stress management tools.

This is a book for anyone concerned with enhancing the lives of children; be they parents, teachers, or others. *Childhood Stress in Contemporary Society* is an invaluable resource that should be read by all adults so they can apply its principles and recommendations to the children with whom they interact."

Jerrold S. Greenberg, EdD
Professor, Department of Public and Community Health,
University of Maryland

The Haworth Press®
New York • London • Oxford

Childhood Stress
in Contemporary Society

Childhood Stress
in Contemporary Society

James H. Humphrey

The Haworth Press®
New York • London • Oxford

The Haworth Press, Inc., 10 Alice Street, Binghamton, NY 13904-1580.

Cover design by Brooke R. Stiles.

Library of Congress Cataloging-in-Publication Data

Humphrey, James Harry, 1911-
    Childhood stress in contemporary society / James H. Humphrey.
        p. cm.
    Includes bibliographical references and index.
    ISBN 0-7890-2265-6 (hard : alk. paper)—ISBN 0-7890-2266-4 (pbk. : alk. paper)
    1. Stress in children. 2. Child rearing. I. Title.
BF723.S75H842 2004
155.4'18—dc22
                                                                        2003025570

CONTENTS

ABOUT THE AUTHOR

James H. Humphrey, EdD, is Professor Emeritus at the University of Maryland. Dr. Humphrey has authored or co-authored more than 60 books, including *Stress in College Athletics: Causes, Consequences, Coping* (Haworth), and edited 43 others. Considered a pioneer in stress education, he is the founder and editor of *Human Stress: Current Selected Research* and editor of the 16-book series on Stress in Modern Society. His writings and research reports have appeared in more than 20 national and international journals and magazines, and he is listed in the *International Authors and Writers Who's Who* and *Contemporary Authors of Meritorious Works*. In the early 1980s, Dr. Humphrey collaborated with the late Hans Selye, who is generally known as the "Father of Stress." Dr. Humphrey has received numerous honors and awards. He is a Fellow in the American Institute of Stress.

Foreword

Numerous statistics confirm that stress levels have risen progressively over the past few decades. Job pressures have been emphasized as the greatest source of stress for American adults. Other demographic groups also have been affected by job stress as well as other issues. For the elderly, these include such obvious problems as increased social isolation and mental and physical disabilities. Children, however, are influenced by a host of other interrelated issues, which are more covert, complex, and insidious. In addition, unlike other groups, children may not be aware that they are suffering from stress-related symptoms and are unable to voice their complaints as effectively as adults because usually they are not organized as a group. Stress has now reached pandemic proportions in children, largely because of changes in the way they are being educated and reared.

Television has become a particularly disruptive force because of its emphasis on and sometimes glorification of violence and crime. Forty percent of households now have three or more TVs and more than 400,000 "mobile video units" were installed in cars last year, particularly SUVs and minivans, with some having two sets. The average American one-year-old now watches six hours of TV weekly and the amount of time the average youth spends watching television exceeds the amount of time spent in school by 100 hours. By age thirteen, a child will have witnessed more than 52,000 murders, rapes, armed robberies, and assaults on television. The number rises to 75,000 for those with cable or satellite receivers. Studies have shown that TV violence may be responsible for more than half of the murders committed in the United States. When South Africa banned television between 1945 and 1975, the homicide rate dropped 7 percent while it rose in other countries. After the relegalization of television, homicides shot up 130 percent within twelve years. Television programs also paint a warped portrait of adult life that has replaced conventional role models with unrealistic heroes and occupations that some kids aspire to, such as Terminator, Ninja Turtle, Ghostbuster, Batman, and Star Trek Commander. Protracted TV watching, with its associated fast-food snacking and increased secretion of stress hormones, is believed by many to be a significant factor in the current epidemic of childhood obesity and even type II, or adult-onset diabetes.

A February 18, 2003, Florida newspaper item indicated that a fifteen-year-old boy sentenced to life imprisonment for killing an eighty-three-year-old widow in 1977 in a botched burglary attempt was now scheduled to be released in 2005 instead of 2012 due to good behavior. The case attracted national attention because it was one of the first to be broadcast live after cameras were allowed in the courtroom and the unusual defense of "television intoxication" failed to sway a jury. The boy's attorney claimed the defendant was legally insane at the time of the killing because "he was brainwashed by years of watching violence on television." Some of the popular shows cited included *Kojak, The Rockford Files, Mannix, Baretta, The Streets of San Francisco, Starsky & Hutch,* and *The Dukes of Hazzard.* Today, TV viewers are fed a steady diet of make-believe murderers and detectives with some, such as *CSI,* retracing the steps from a bloody autopsy to a vivid reenactment of the violent crime. New entertainment technology has also brought an explosion of violent video games, perhaps the most shocking of which, *Grand Theft Auto 3,* features a character who murders prostitutes with a baseball bat. It has become one of the most popular titles in this $20 billion global industry.

Children tend to imitate what they see on TV, which can have disastrous results even if a program is not rated as violent. Another report in the same February 18, 2003, newspaper stated that, "A thirteen-year-old boy described as an excellent swimmer drowned while playing an endurance game he and his friends called 'Mission'." The game was based on a scene from the movie *Blue Crush* about a women's surfing competition in which a girl in training holds a large rock while running on the ocean bottom and surfaces gasping for air. When the thirteen-year-old was pulled from the bottom of a pond, he "still had a heavy tow chain twisted three times around his chest and waist." Other neighborhood children, one of whom was nine years old, had also tried swimming across the pond with a baby stroller and other items but gave up. A previous Florida drowning death of an autistic five-year-old was blamed on a seventeen-year-old who had been "imitating The Rock" (Dwayne Johnson) on a professional wrestling TV show. A nine- and ten-year-old who had witnessed the event testified at the trial that they and the victim had watched a program featuring The Rock two days previously and that after the defendant had pushed the deceased into the canal he "walked away laughing as the boy struggled." The prosecutor emphasized that "Little boys imitate what they see on TV. If they hadn't been watching the wrestling, none of this might have happened." The defendant could receive up to thirty years in prison but the two younger boys were offered immunity for their testimony. Pro wrestling came up last year in another Florida trial when a fourteen-year-old boy was sentenced to life in prison for killing his six-year-old playmate. His attorney had argued that the death was an accident and that the accused was simply practicing wrestling moves the children had seen on television.

Childhood, as we formerly recognized it, has practically become extinct. Less and less leisure time exists for playing with others and learning how to develop friendships and social skills. Creative, constructive, and relaxing activities such as painting or making things with erector sets or Lincoln Logs are now passé, if not obsolete. These have been replaced by fast-paced, stressful, competitive video games that focus on destructive acts, such as killing as many opponents as possible in the shortest period of time. It is now not unusual to see fierce competition, aggression, time urgency, and other manifestations of Type A coronary-prone behavior at the nursery school level, anxiety attacks at age nine, and even ulcers in children under the age of twelve.

Superimposed on this has been the continued disintegration of traditional family life and the powerful stress-busting benefits provided by a strong social support system. More than half of American marriages now end in divorce, which can have dire effects on more than one million children. More than half of all whites and three out of four African Americans under age eighteen will spend part of their life in a single-parent household. Forty percent of children are born to single mothers, a similar number have no health insurance, and almost half under the age of six live below the poverty level.

Many people feel that factors such as increased disruptive family life, parental abuse, and TV programs that lead to peer pressure are the major reasons the United States has the highest teen pregnancy rates in Western society. Such influences may also help to explain why teen suicide and homicide rates have tripled over the past three decades. Homicide by firearms is the leading cause of death in fifteen- to nineteen-year-old African Americans and is exceeded only by automobile accidents and suicides for Caucasians in the same age group. Acquired immunodeficiency syndrome (AIDS) is also spreading faster in this segment of the population than in any other age group, as are substance abuse, alcoholism, and drug addiction.

The root cause of most of these problems might be the loneliness that stems from social isolation and/or of the lack of ability to communicate with others due to educational deficiencies. As James Lynch points out in *A Cry Unheard* (2000), loneliness in childhood has "a significant impact on the incidence of serious disease and premature death decades later in adulthood." School failure can be a major contributor to this problem because these children become more socially isolated and deficient in the language and communication skills that could help them overcome their isolation. This is particularly true for minority groups who have the highest school drop-out rates and more severe social isolation and loneliness because of language difficulties that hinder effective communication. Follow-up studies show that such individuals die at significantly higher rates decades later not only from premature coronary heart disease but also disorders ranging from cancer and Alzheimer's disease to tuberculosis and mental illness. As I have discussed elsewhere and Lynch so eloquently explains, we need to recognize that loneliness due to communicative deficiencies might be even more deadly than communicable diseases, for which drugs are readily available.

No easy solutions or quick fixes exist for these growing societal ills. However, many can be prevented or reduced by making parents, family members, teachers, religious counselors, and others aware of the causes and serious consequences of childhood stress and educating them about early warning signs and what steps can be taken to reduce stress levels among children. Dr. Humphrey has had extensive experience in these areas, and his book goes a long way in fulfilling this need.

Paul J. Rosch, MD, FACP
President, The American Institute of Stress;
Clinical Professor of Medicine and Psychiatry,
New York Medical College

Introduction

Over the past several years literally thousands of items of literature in different forms have been published on various aspects of stress. No doubt this attests to the notion that this area of health concern may well be one of the most important in modern times. It is interesting to note, however, that this abundance of literature has pertained essentially to the adult population. That is, it has appeared generally that stress mainly affects adults.

With discoveries indicating that stress among adults is likely to have its roots in childhood, much more attention is currently being directed toward dealing with stress in children. My good friend, the late Hans Selye (generally known as the "Father of Stress") when we were collaborating on a childhood stress research project remarked to me: "I think it is extremely important to begin teaching the stress concept to children at a very early age, because all codes of behavior sink in best if a tradition is established" (personal communication, 1980).

Two decades ago, on the basis of my own examination of more than 3,000 items of literature on stress, I estimated that only 10 to 12 percent of it was devoted to childhood stress. In a similar examination in the past year I found that as much as 20 to 25 percent of such literature now pertains to stress among children.

It has become even more important because it has now been clearly demonstrated that children who associate with stressed adults are very likely to become stress ridden themselves. Herein lies the importance of this book, the purpose of which is to teach adults how they can cope with their own stress and how to deal with stress in children.

The book is directed to those adults who are engaged in some way with children—parents, teachers, counselors, and other adult friends. Its purpose is to help adults themselves understand and to be able to help children understand about stress and how to control it.

As previously mentioned, although we tend to think of undesirable stress as being mainly concerned with the adult population, it can have a devastating effect on growing children. If valid information can be provided for adults who deal with children perhaps they will be not only better prepared to understand stress, but will be able to help children deal with it as well.

The need for a book of this nature is clearly demonstrated by the fact that increasing evidence shows that children supervised by adults who themselves do not cope well with stress also will have difficulty coping. In addition, it has been found that when these same adults improve their own ability to control stress, this skill is also passed along to children.

As will be discussed later, there are many causes of stress; almost anything that occurs in life can induce stress to some degree. Various factors of our modern, highly technological society, including the mass media (especially the daily news, which bombards us with information), overcrowding, air and noise pollution, and the everyday "hustle and bustle to survive" can combine to make life a somewhat frustrating experience. All of us, children and adults alike, are potential stress victims of the kinds of conditions previously mentioned.

Most children encounter a considerable amount of undesirable stress in our complex modern society. One of the problems of stress in children is that they are not likely to be able to cope with it as well as adults. One reason for this is that they do not have the readily available options that adults might have. In fact, many prominent child psychologists have made the following comparisons between choices available to children and adults when coping with stress.

1. An open display of anger is often considered unacceptable for children. For example, a teacher can be angry with students, but children may not have the same right to be angry with a teacher.
2. Adults can withdraw or walk out, but this same option of freedom is not likely to be available to children.
3. An adult can get a prescription for "nerves" from a physician— another option not available to children.
4. It is very likely that more often than not children will be punished for using some of the same kinds of stress-coping techniques that are acceptable for adults, most of which are considered socially unacceptable for children.

Perhaps at this point I should identify the population with which this book is primarily concerned. That is, what is meant by the term *children,* particularly with reference to age range? In this regard the concern is essentially with children from approximately age two to age twelve, or from the time children are eligible to enter preschool until they complete elementary school.

I hasten to mention that stress can occur prior to two years of age. For example, it is the general belief that infants are unaware of the differences between self and the physical and human environment. Many child development specialists feel that the two most important tasks of the infant and child up to the age of two are to establish inner images of the outer world of people and objects. In the process of establishing such images life can be unpleasant for this age range and as a result may become stressful.

It should be clarified that it is not absolutely necessary for everyone to be an expert in behavior therapy in order to deal with stress in childhood. Most adults can apply certain general principles in helping to control stress. These principles are presented here to set the stage for a better understanding of the theme and content of this book.

1. *Personal health practices should be carefully observed.* This is an easy principle to accept, but it is not always easy to put into action. No one is against health but not everyone abides by those practices that can help to maintain a suitable level of health. Parents in particular should accept the major share of the responsibility for health practices of children. In doing so, they can help to eliminate unacceptable health behaviors, relating such behaviors to stress.

2. *Make a continuous effort to take stock of ourselves.* The practice of constantly taking stock of one's activities can help to minimize many problems. This can be accomplished in part by taking a little time at the end of each day for an evaluation of the events that occurred during the day and reactions to those events. Adults should give serious consideration to this practice and attempt to guide children in a direction that will help them understand why they may have become upset over an incident that happened during the day.

3. *Learn to recognize your own accomplishments.* One must learn to recognize his or her own accomplishments and praise himself or herself for them, especially if such praise is not offered by others. This is generally known as "stroking" or "patting one's self on the back." In practicing this procedure adults can de-

velop positive attitudes and/or belief systems about their own accomplishments and thus reduce stress. At the same time they can try to instill this idea into the lives of children.

4. *Learn to take one thing at a time.* This principle concerns time budgeting and procrastination. Sometimes, both adults and children are likely to procrastinate and, as a consequence, frustration can build up as tasks mount. A need exists to sort out those tasks in order of importance and deal with them one at a time. Proper budgeting of time can help to eliminate worries of time urgency and the feeling of having too much to do and not enough time.

5. *Learn to take things less seriously.* This should not be interpreted to mean that such adult responsibilities as parenting and teaching should not be taken seriously. It does mean that a fine line can occur between what is actually serious and what is not. Sometimes when people look back at a particular event, they may wonder how they could have become so excited about it. Those adults who are able to see the humorous side of life tend to look at potentially stressful situations more objectively, and this can assist in keeping stress levels low. This attitude can be conveyed to children.

6. *Do things for others.* We can sometimes take our minds off our own stressful conditions by offering to do something for other people. Children should be taught to develop this concept early in life. When people are helpful to others in attempting to relieve them from stress, they in turn will tend to be relieved of stress themselves. Much research shows that those who volunteer to help others often get as much benefit from this practice as those they help. In this regard, it has been clearly demonstrated that older children who have reading problems improve their own reading ability when they assist younger children with these same problems.

7. *Talk things over with others.* Some individuals tend to keep things to themselves; therefore, they may not be aware that others are disturbed by the same things. Sometimes discussing an issue with a colleague or a spouse can help one see things in a much different light. Children should be encouraged to talk things over with one another as well as with parents, teachers, and other adult friends.

8. *Stress should not be confused with challenge.* Recognizing that stress is a natural phenomenon of life is no doubt one of the first and most important steps in dealing with it. This is a concept that adults should make every effort to develop in children at an early age.

As you read and acquire information presented in this book it is recommended that you consider these general principles as basic guidelines in directing your efforts to dealing with stress among children.

Currently, with so much more attention being directed to childhood stress, various techniques are available for use in assessing stress in children. These include behavioral observations, physiological assessments, adult rating scales, and child self-report inventories. My own means of acquiring important materials for this book involved extensive surveys of and interviews with hundreds of parents, teachers, counselors, and other adults, as well as children themselves. I want to thank all of these individuals who gave generously of their time to provide information that served as a practical database for this book.

Finally, I owe a personal debt of gratitude to Paul J. Rosch, MD, president of the American Institute of Stress, for critically appraising and evaluating the manuscript for clarity and authenticity.

Chapter 1

Stress Terminology

An unbelievable amount of confusion surrounds the meaning of stress and stress-related terms. For this reason, it appears important to attempt to arrive at some operational definitions and descriptions of some of these terms. If this can be accomplished, it will make for much easier communication in dealing with stress. It is the intent of this introductory chapter to provide information that will help to facilitate communication in the area of stress.

An intelligent discussion of any subject should begin with some sort of understanding about the terminology employed or, in other words, the language and vocabulary used to communicate about a given subject. There are several important reasons why a book on stress, in particular, should begin by establishing such a general frame of reference. Perhaps most important, a review of several hundred pieces of literature concerned with stress revealed that the terminology connected with it is voluminous, sometimes contradictory, and, to say the least, rather confusing. Many times, terms with different meanings are likely to be used interchangeably; conversely, the same term may be used under various circumstances to denote several different meanings. That this results in confusion for the reader is obvious, because such usage of terminology is likely to generate a situation of multiple meanings in the general area of stress. In this regard, my interviews and surveys of individuals of all age levels revealed a wide variety of understandings with reference to the meaning of stress.

I am not attempting to develop a set of standardized stress-related terms. This would be nearly impossible. The purpose is for communication only, and limited to the aims of this particular book; if a term is used in the book, you will know what it means. The idea is to try to develop working descriptions of terms for the purpose of communicating with you, the reader. In no sense is it intended to impose a terminology upon you. If you prefer other terms you should feel free to use them in your communication with others.

For the discussion of terminology that follows, there will be an effort to resort in some instances to terms used by various authorities in the field, and in others, insofar as they may be available, to use pure technical definitions. It should be understood that many of the terms have some sort of general meaning. An attempt will be made in some cases to start with this general meaning and give it specificity for the subject at hand.

STRESS

There is no solid agreement regarding the derivation of the term stress. For example, it is possible that the term is derived from the Latin word *stringere,* which means to "bind tightly." Or it could have derived from the French word *détresse* anglicized to *distress.* The prefix *dis* could eventually have been eliminated because of slurring, as in the case of the word *because* sometimes becoming *'cause.*

A common generalized literal description of stress is "a constraining force or influence." When applied to the human organism, this could be interpreted to mean the extent to which the body can withstand a given force or influence. In this regard, one of the most often quoted descriptions of stress is that of the famous pioneer in the field, the late Hans Selye, who described it as the "non-specific response of the body to any demand made upon it."[1] This means that stress involves a mobilization of the body's resources in response to a stimulus (stressor). These responses can include various physical and chemical changes in the organism. This description of stress could be extended by stating that it involves demands that tax or exceed the resources of the human organism. This means that stress not only involves these bodily responses but that it also involves wear and tear, brought about by these responses, on the organism. (Selye's concept of stress will be explained in more detail in Chapter 2.)

Stress can be considered as any factor, acting internally or externally, that makes it difficult to adapt and that indicates increased effort on the part of the individual to maintain a state of equilibrium between himself or herself and the external environment. It is emphasized that stress is a *state* that one is in, and this should not be confused with any *agent* that produces such a state. Such agents are referred to as stressors.

Understanding the meaning of stress can be made more difficult because certain stress-related terms can cause confusion. Therefore, it seems appropriate at this point to review the meanings of such terms as tension, emotion, anxiety, burnout, and depression.

TENSION

The term tension is very frequently used in relation to stress, and thus attention should be given to the meaning of this term. It is interesting to examine the entries used for these terms in the *Education Index*. This bibliographical index of periodical educational literature records entries on the terms stress and tension as follows:

> *Stress* (physiology)
> *Stress* (psychology) see *Tension* (psychology)
> *Tension* (physiology) see *Stress* (physiology)
> *Tension* (psychology)

These entries indicate that stress and tension have both physiological and psychological aspects. However, articles in the periodical literature listed as "stress" articles seem to imply that stress is more physiologically oriented and that tension is more psychologically oriented. Thus, psychological stress and physiological tension could be interpreted to mean the same thing. The breakdown in this position is seen in another entry for tension, which is concerned with *muscular* tension. The latter, of course, must be considered to have a physiological orientation. In the final analysis, the validity of these entries will depend upon the point of view of each individual. As we shall discover later in the book, the validity of this particular cataloging of these terms may possibly be at odds with a more specific meaning of the term.

Tensions can be viewed in two frames of reference; first, as *physiologic* or *unlearned tensions,* and second, as *psychologic* or *learned tensions.* An example of the first, physiological or unlearned tensions would be "tensing" at bright lights or intense sounds. Psychologic or learned tensions are responses to stimuli that ordinarily do not involve muscular contractions, but that at some time earlier in a person's experience were associated with a situation in which tension was a part of the normal response. Because the brain connects any events that stimulate it simultaneously, it would appear that, depending upon the unlimited kinds of personal experiences one might have, he or she may show tension to any and all kinds of stimuli. An example of a psychologic or learned tension would be an inability to relax when riding in a car after experiencing or imagining too many automobile accidents.

In a sense, it may be inferred that physiologic or unlearned tensions are current and spontaneous, while psychologic or learned tensions may be latent as a result of a previous experience and may emerge at a later time. Although there may be a hairline distinction between stress and tension in the minds of some people, perhaps an essential difference between stress and tension is that the former is a physical and/or mental state concerned with wear and tear on the organism, while the latter is either a spontaneous or latent condition which can bring about this wear and tear.

EMOTION

Since the terms stress and emotion are used interchangeably in some of the literature, consideration should be given to the meaning of the latter term. Emotion can be viewed as the response an individual makes when confronted with a situation for which he or she is unprepared or which is interpreted as a possible source of gain or loss. For example, if one is confronted with a situation for which he or she may not have a satisfactory response, the emotional pattern of fear could result. Or, if a person's desires are frustrated, the emotional pattern of anger may occur. Emotion, then, is not the state of stress itself, but is a stressor that can stimulate stress. (The subject of childhood emotions will be discussed in detail in Chapter 3.)

ANXIETY

Anxiety is another term often used to mean the same as stress. In fact, some of the literature uses the expression "anxiety *or* stress," implying that they are the same. This can lead to the "chicken-and-egg" controversy. Is stress the cause of anxiety or is anxiety the cause of stress? Or, is it a reciprocal situation?

A basic literal meaning of anxiety is "uneasiness of the mind," but this simple generalization may be more complex than one might think. C. Eugene Walker, a notable clinical psychologist and a contributor to my Human Stress Series, points out that psychologists who deal with this area in detail have difficulty defining the term. He gives his own description of it as the "reaction to a situation where we believe our well-being is endangered or threatened in some way."[2] David Viscott, another authoritative source, considers anxiety as the "fear of hurt or loss." He contends that this leads to anger, with anger leading to guilt which, if unrelieved, leads to depression.[3]

BURNOUT

Some persons become unable to cope with the physical and emotional trauma generated by the demands of their energy, emotions, and time. Current research conducted on people-oriented occupations indicates that some occupations are characterized by several built-in sources of frustration, that eventually lead dedicated workers to become ineffective and apathetic, that is, burned out. Persons who experience burnout may begin to perceive their job as impossible. They may begin to question their ability. Feeling helpless and out of control, persons nearing burnout may tire easily and may experience headaches and/or digestive problems. In some cases they will view their tasks and their profession to be increasingly meaningless, trivial, or irrelevant.

With regard to burnout, a study of college athletes by William C. Thomas and colleagues is of interest.[4] They hypothesized that the personality trait known as *hardiness* could mediate the effects of stress that lead to burnout. They also hypothesized that hardiness is one characteristic that could differentiate between individuals who are able to effectively manage environmental and internal demands and those who burn out.

The purpose of the study was to examine a theoretical model in which hardiness was posited to act as a stress buffer in the stress-burnout relationship. Participants were 181 National Collegiate Athletic Association Division I athletes who completed questionnaires containing stress, hardiness, and burnout instruments.

The study revealed that hardiness did appear to act as a buffer against the effects of stress. Given the positive consequences of having a hardier personality, it was concluded that athletes could benefit from purposefully structured experiences to enhance hardiness and improve their ability to cope with the many situational demands placed on them.

DEPRESSION

The term depression, as used here, is thought of as a painful emotional reaction characterized by intense feelings of loss, sadness, worthlessness, failure, or rejection not warranted by an objective view of events. Depression is often a disproportionately intense reaction to difficult life situations. It may be accompanied by such physiological symptoms as tension, slowing of motor and mental activity, fatigue, lack of appetite, and insomnia, that is, some of the same symptoms accompanying undesirable stress.

Depression can be a manifestation of many different psychomotor and physical disorders and a normal response to certain types of stress. Unless the cause of it can be clearly identified, depression usually represents a description rather than a diagnosis.

An estimated 15 percent of the population develops an episode of depression requiring medical intervention at some point in life, and stress is not the only cause.[5] Some people are born with a biological predisposition to depression, tending toward a brain chemical imbalance that favors a depressed mental state. In some situations the depression appears to come from nowhere, even in the best circumstances. Perhaps more frequently, the depression stems from a combination of stressful life events and internal biological factors.

Although this brief discussion of terms does not exhaust the vocabulary used in relation to stress, it will serve to help the reader distinguish the use of terms basic to an understanding of stress. Other terminology will be described as needed when dealing with specific topics in subsequent discussions.

Chapter 2

All About Stress

Stress! What is it? How do we react to it? What causes it? How does it affect us? Is it all bad? Answers to questions such as these are helpful if adults are to achieve any degree of success in their efforts to control stress in children. That is, they should have some awareness of just what it is they are trying to control. Therefore, it is the function of this chapter to provide the reader with an overview of some of the various aspects of stress. More specific ways adults can help children understand the complex nature of stress will be discussed in Chapter 4.

It should be mentioned that it is not the intent of this book to undertake a highly technical discourse on the complex nature of stress. However, certain basic understandings need to be taken into account, and this requires the use of certain technical terms. For this reason, it appears appropriate to provide an "on-the-spot" glossary of terms used in the discussion to follow.

> *ACTH:* AdrenoCorticoTropic Hormone is secreted by the pituitary gland. It influences the function of the adrenals and other glands in the body.
>
> *Adrenalin:* A hormone secreted by the medulla of the adrenal glands.
>
> *Adrenals:* Two glands in the upper posterior part of the abdomen that produce and secrete hormones. They have two parts, the outer layer, called the *cortex* and the inner core called the *medulla.*
>
> *Corticoids:* Hormones produced by the adrenal cortex, an example of which is *cortisone.*
>
> *Endocrine:* Glands that secrete their hormones into the bloodstream.

Hormone: A chemical produced by a gland, secreted into the bloodstream, and influencing the function of cells or organs.

Hypothalamus: The primary activator of the autonomic nervous system, it plays a central role in translating neurological stimuli into endocrine processes during stress reactions.

Pituitary: An endocrine gland located at the base of the brain about the size of a pea. It secretes important hormones, one of which is ACTH.

Thymus: A ductless gland that is considered a part of the endocrine gland system, located behind the upper part of the breast bone.

Although there are various theories of stress, Hans Selye provides one of the better known and widely accepted ones.[1] Selye's description of stress has already been given as the "nonspecific response of the body to any demand made upon it." The physiological processes and the reactions involved in Selye's stress model is known as the general adaptation syndrome and consists of three stages: *alarm reaction, resistance,* and *exhaustion.*

In the first stage (alarm reaction), the body reacts to the stressor and causes the hypothalamus to produce a biochemical "messenger," which in turn causes the pituitary gland to secrete ACTH into the blood. This hormone then causes the adrenal gland to discharge adrenalin and other corticoids. This causes shrinkage of the thymus with an influence on heart rate, blood pressure, etc. It is during the alarm stage that the resistance of the body is reduced.

In the second stage, resistance develops if the stressor is not too pronounced. Body adaptation develops to fight back the stress or possibly avoid it, and the body begins to repair damage, if any.

The third stage of exhaustion occurs if there is long continued exposure to the same stressor. The ability of adaptation is eventually exhausted and the signs of the first stage (alarm reaction) reappear. Selye contended that our adaptation resources are limited and when they become irreversible, the result is death. Our objective, of course, should be to keep our resistance and capacity for adaptation.

Selye's stress model, which places emphasis upon nonspecific responses, has been widely accepted. However, the nonspecific nature of stress has been questioned by some. This means that psychological stressors activate other endocrine systems in addition to those activated by physiological stressors such as cold and electric shock.

As in the case of all research, the search for truth will continue, and more precise and sophisticated procedures will emerge in the scientific study of stress. Current theories will be more critically appraised and evaluated and other theories may continue to be advanced. In the meantime, there is abundant evidence to support the notion that if not controlled, stress in modern society is a most serious threat to the well-being of man. Of course, the most important factor in such control is man himself.

REACTIONS TO STRESS

Reactions to stress may be classified in various ways and, in any classification some degree of unavoidable overlapping occurs. In the discussion here, I arbitrarily suggest two broad classifications as *physiological* and *behavioral*.

Physiological Reactions

Although all individuals do not always react to stress in the same way physiologically, the following general list suggests some of the more or less standard body reactions.

1. Rapid heartbeat, which has sometimes been described as "pounding of the heart." Most of us have experienced this reaction as a result of great excitement, or as a result of being afraid.
2. Perspiration, which is mostly of the palms, although profuse sweating may occur in some individuals in other parts of the body.
3. The blood pressure rises, which may be referred to as a hidden reaction because the individual is not likely to be aware of it.
4. The pupils of the eyes may dilate and, again, the individual will not necessarily be aware of it.
5. The stomach seems to "knot up," and this is described as "feeling a lump in the pit of the stomach." This can have a negative influence on digestion.
6. Sometimes individuals experience difficulty in swallowing, often characterized as a "lump in the throat."

7. There may be a "tight" feeling in the chest and when the stress-ful condition is relieved one may refer to it as "getting a load off my chest."

These various bodily reactions indicate that the organism is gear-ing up for a response to a stressor. This phenomenon is called the *fight-or-flight* response and was first described as an emergency reac-tion by Walter B. Cannon,[2] the famous Harvard University professor of physiology. The fight-or-flight response prepares us for action in the same way prehistoric man reacted when confronted with an en-emy. His responses were based on the particular situation, such as fighting an opponent for food or fleeing from an animal that provided him with an overmatched situation. In modern times, with all of the potentially stressful conditions that provoke a fight-or-flight response, modern man uses these same physiological responses to face up to these situations. Today, we generally do not need to fight physically (although we might feel like it sometimes) or run from wild animals, but our bodies still react with the same fight-or-flight response. Phys-iologists point out that we still need this means of self-preservation occasionally, but not in response to the emotional traumas and anxi-eties of modern living.

Behavioral Reactions

In discussing behavioral reactions, it should be mentioned again that various degrees of unavoidable overlapping may occur between these reactions and physiological reactions. For purposes of this dis-cussion, I will consider *behavior* to mean anything that the organism does as a result of stimulation.

An individual under stress will function with a behavior that is dif-ferent from ordinary behavior. These are subclassified as: (1) *counter* behavior (sometimes referred to as defensive behavior), (2) *dysfunc-tional* behavior, and (3) *overt* behavior (sometimes referred to as ex-pressive behavior).

In counter behavior, a person sometimes takes action that is in-tended to counteract the stressful condition. For example, an individ-ual may take a defensive position by practicing an "on-the-spot" relaxation technique, but at the same time may be unaware of it. He or she may take a deep breath and silently count to ten before taking ac-tion, if any.

Dysfunctional behavior means that a person will react in a manner that demonstrates impaired or abnormal functioning, which results in a lower level of skill performance than he or she is ordinarily capable of accomplishing. Changes in the speech pattern and a temporary loss of memory may occur. Many of us have experienced these problems due to a stress-inducing situation, with a mental block causing some degree of frustration while we attempt to recover the original train of thought.

Overt behavior involves such reactions as distorted facial expressions, that is, tics and twitches and biting the lip. The person needs to move about, therefore pacing around the room is characteristic of this condition. Incidentally, one point of view suggests that overt behavior in the form of activity is preferable for most individuals in most stressful situations, and can be highly effective in reducing threat and distress.

CLASSIFICATIONS OF STRESS

The difficulty encountered in attempting to devise a foolproof classification system for the various kinds of stress should be obvious; it is practically impossible to fit a given type of stress into one exclusive category because of the possibility of overlapping. As in the case of attempting to classify reactions to stress in the previous discussion, we are confronted with the same problem in trying to classify various kinds of stress. However, an attempt will be made to do so and, as mentioned before, any such classification on the part of the author is arbitrary. Others may wish to use different classifications than those used here and in the absence of anything resembling standardization, it is their prerogative to do so. With this idea in mind, some general classifications of stress that will be dealt with in the following discussion are: (1) desirable and undesirable stress, (2) physical stress, (3) psychological stress, and (4) social stress. This particular listing is not necessarily theoretically complete, but for the purposes of this book it should suffice.

Desirable and Undesirable Stress

The classic comment once made by Selye that "stress is the spice of life" sums up the idea that stress can be desirable as well as devastating. He went on to say that the only way one could avoid stress would be to never do anything and that certain kinds of activities have a beneficial influence in keeping the stress mechanism in good shape. Certainly the human organism needs to be taxed in order to function well, and it is a well-known physiological fact that muscles will soon atrophy if not subjected to sufficient use.

At one time or another most of us have experienced "butterflies in the stomach" when faced with a particularly challenging situation. Thus, it is important that we understand that stress is a perfectly normal human state and that the organism is under various degrees of stress in conditions related to happiness as well as those concerned with sadness.

In the literature, undesirable stress may be referred to as *distress*. It is interesting to note that Selye referred to the pleasant or healthy kind of stress as *eustress* and to the unpleasant or unhealthy kind as *distress*.

Some of the desirable features of stress have been mentioned, but similar to any factor involving the human organism, anything in excess can have a negative effect. When stress becomes prolonged and unrelenting (chronic), it can result in serious trouble. In the final analysis, the recommendation is not necessarily to avoid stress, but to keep it from becoming a chronic condition.

Although both *good* stress and *bad* stress reactions place specific demands for resources on the body, does this mean that good stress is *safe* and bad stress is dangerous? Two prominent psychologists, Israel Posner and Lewis Leitner[3] have made some interesting suggestions in this regard. They feel that two psychological variables, *predictability* and *controllability,* play an important role. Let us examine this premise.

It can be reasoned that predictable pain and discomfort is less stressful because under this condition a person could be capable of learning when it is safe to lower his or her guard and relax. Since periods of impending pain are clearly signaled, the person can safely relax at times when the warning is absent. These periods of psychological safety seem to insulate individuals from harmful effects of stress. Obviously, persons receiving unsignaled pain have no way of knowing when it is safe to relax and are more likely to develop serious health problems as a result of chronic psychological stress.

The second psychological variable, controllability of environmental stressors, which is closely related to coping behavior, also plays a major role in determining stress effects. The ability to control painful events may insulate individuals from experiencing damaging stress effects. However, such coping behavior is beneficial only if a person is given feedback signals that inform him or her that the coping response was successful in avoiding an impending stressor. Without the feedback of success, active coping behavior, as such, may increase stress effects since it calls upon the energy reserves of the body and leaves it in a state of chronic stress.

The research on predictability and controllability of stressful events may help to answer *why* people who seek out stressful and challenging types of jobs do not appear to develop stress illnesses from this form of stress. In contrast, when essentially similar body reactivity is produced by bad stress, then stress-related illnesses can be the result. Perhaps good stress does not produce illness because typically the events associated with it are planned in advance (they are predictable) or otherwise scheduled to integrate (they are controlled) into the individual's life. However, even activities that are generally considered to be pleasant and exciting (good stress) can produce illness if the individual is not forewarned or has little control over the events. In addition, unpleasant events (bad stress) may result in stress-related illness because they generally occur without warning and cannot be controlled.

Some persons have taken the middle ground on this subject by stating that stress is neither good nor bad, indicating that the effect of stress is not determined by the stress itself but how it is viewed and handled. We either handle stress properly or we allow it to influence us negatively and thus become victims of undesirable stress.

Physical Stress

In discussing physical stress it is important to differentiate between the two terms *physical* and *physiological*. The former should be considered a broad term and can be described as "pertaining or relating to the body." On the other hand, physiological is concerned with what the organs do in relation to one another. Therefore, physical stress could be concerned with unusual and excessive physical exertion, as well as certain physiological conditions brought about by stress.

Physical stress can be separated into two general types, to which the organism may react in different ways. One type may be referred to as *emergency* stress and the other as *continued* stress. In emergency stress, when an emergency such as bodily injury arises, hormones are discharged into the bloodstream. This involves an increase in heart rate, rise in blood pressure, and dilations of the blood vessels in the muscles to prepare themselves for immediate use of the generated energy.

In continuing stress, the body's reaction is somewhat more complex. The physiological involvement is the same, but more and more hormones continue to be produced, the purpose of which is to increase body resistance. In cases of excessive stress, such as an extensive third-degree burn, a third phase in the form of exhaustion of the adrenal glands can develop, sometimes culminating in fatality.

Physical stress can also be concerned with unusual and excessive physical exertion. This can be depicted in a general way by performing an experiment involving some mild physical exertion. First, try to find your resting pulse. This can be done by placing your right wrist, palm facing you, in your left hand. Now, bring the index and middle fingers of your left hand around the wrist and press lightly until you feel the beat of your pulse. Next, time this beat for ten seconds and then multiply this by six. This will give you your resting pulse rate per minute. For example, if you counted twelve beats in ten seconds, your resting pulse will be seventy-two beats per minute. The next step is to engage in some physical activity. Stand and balance yourself on one foot. Hop up and down on this foot for a period of about fifteen seconds, or less if it is too strenuous. Take your pulse rate again in the same manner. As a result of this activity, your pulse will be elevated above your resting pulse. Even with this small amount of physical exertion, the body adjusted to cope with it, as evidenced by the rise in pulse rate. This was discernible to you; however, other factors, such as a slight rise in blood pressure, were likely involved and you were not aware of them.

Psychological Stress

The essential difference between physical stress and psychological stress is that the former involves a real situation, while psychological stress is more concerned with foreseeing or imagining an emergency situation. As an example, a vicarious experience of danger may be of sufficient intensity to cause muscle tension and elevate the heart rate. "Stage fright" is a specific example of psychological stress. Interestingly, this type of psychological stress may start when one is a child. For example, my studies of stress-inducing factors among children have indicated that getting up in front of the class is an incident that causes much concern and worry for a large number of children. My experience indicates that this condition also prevails with many adults. It has been clearly demonstrated that prolonged and unrelenting nervous tension developing from psychological stress can result in psychosomatic disorders, which in turn can cause various serious diseases.

Physiological and psychological conceptions of stress have evolved independently within their respective fields. One writer on the subject, Anis Mikhail, once proposed the following holistic definition of stress for the purpose of emphasizing the continuity between psychological and physiological theorizing: "Stress is a state which arises from an actual or perceived demand-capability imbalance in the organism's vital adjustment actions, and which is partially manifested by a nonspecific response."[4]

Social Stress

Humans are social beings. They play together. They work together for the benefit of society. They have fought together in times of national emergencies to preserve the kind of society in which they believe. This means that life involves a constant series of social interactions. These interactions involve a two-way street: the individual has some sort of impact upon society and, in turn, society has an influence upon the individual. Obviously, many levels of social stress exist in life situations. For example, adverse economic conditions and other social problems cause stress for many people.

Negative attitudes about social interactions will almost always generate hard feelings and hostility among groups, causing more stressful conditions for all concerned. A neutral or laissez-faire attitude often degenerates into tolerance and can become almost as devastating as a negative attitude. In fact, the development of an "I don't care" attitude can often make life intolerable and bring about stress. People themselves hold the key to avoidance of undesirable social stress in any kind of environment, and good social relationships are more likely to be obtained if one assumes a positive attitude in such relationships.

CAUSES OF STRESS

A fair question to raise might be, "What doesn't cause stress?" This is mentioned because most human environments, including the workplace and society as a whole, are now seen as stress inducing to some degree. In recent years so many causes of cancer have been advanced that many persons have almost come to the conclusion that *everything* causes cancer. Perhaps the same could be said of stress. Because it has reached near-epidemic proportions, it is easy to believe that *everything* causes stress.

Factors that induce stress are likely to be both general and specific. Major life events can be stress inducing. Also, in our day-to-day environments, many specific causes of stress can elevate undesirable stress levels.

A number of researchers have studied certain *life events* as causes of stress. They have attempted to find out what kinds of health problems are associated with various events, normal and abnormal, that afflict people either in the usual course of events or as a result of some sort of misfortune. One of the best known studies is the early original work of T. H. Holmes and R. H. Rahe[5]—a social readjustment ratings scale. Following is a list of the authors' ten most serious stress-inducing events.

1. Death of a spouse
2. Divorce
3. Marital separation
4. Jail term
5. Death of a close family member
6. Personal injury

7. Marriage
8. Dismissal from work
9. Marital reconciliation
10. Retirement

As important as life events scales are as a means of determining causes of stress, some specialists feel that another good measure is that which is concerned with day-to-day problems. Prominent in this regard is Richard Lazarus,[6] the distinguished stress researcher at the University of California at Berkeley. He and his associates once collected data from a number of populations to identify "daily hassles." Following is the list of hassles for one of these populations—100 white, middle-class, middle-aged men and women.

1. Concern about weight
2. Health of a family member
3. Rising prices of common goods
4. Home maintenance
5. Too many things to do
6. Yard work or outdoor maintenance
7. Property, investment, or taxes
8. Crime
9. Physical appearance

Some Causes of Stress Among Children

As previously mentioned, during the past several years various researchers have studied life events and daily hassles as causes of stress. As far as life events are concerned, the following appear to be the most prevalent in childhood.

1. The death of a parent
2. The death of a sibling
3. Divorce of parents
4. Marital separation of parents
5. The death of a grandparent
6. Hospitalization of a parent
7. Remarriage of a parent
8. Birth of a sibling

9. Hospitalization of a sibling
10. Loss of a job by mother or father

In the area of daily hassles in my own studies of childhood stress, I have collected data on daily stressors of children in four different age ranges. Following are the five most common daily hassles of children at these ages.

Ages Five to Six

Fighting with my brother
Not knowing what I should do
Starting school
When I have to go to bed early
Having to eat stuff I don't like

Ages Seven to Eight

When my parents don't trust me
When my mother blames me for something I didn't do
Afraid I will fail
Kids who don't like me
Having to do homework

Ages Nine to Ten

When I can't watch TV
When teachers don't treat me like a person
When I don't get credit for something I did
Unfair punishment
Parents who think they know everything

Ages Eleven to Twelve

Teachers who think they know it all
Not being as strong as I would like to be
Girls who think they are smart
Kids who make fun of me
Wearing my older brother's clothes

Obviously, most of these daily hassles can be dealt with in a suitable manner by alert adults. These are general causes of stress; more specific causes will emerge in subsequent discussions.

EFFECTS OF STRESS

The viewpoint that prompts the comment "almost everything causes stress," could be applied with the assertion that stress causes everything. A tragic consequence is that stress-related psychological and physiological disorders are viewed as primary social and health problems. Compelling evidence from studies and clinical trials, as well as many standard medical textbooks, attributes anywhere from 50 to 80 percent of all diseases, at least in part, to stress-related origins.

The literature by various medical authorities shows that among other conditions, the following in some way could be stress related: diabetes, cirrhosis of the liver, high blood pressure, peptic ulcer, migraine headaches, multiple sclerosis, lung disease, injury due to accidents, mental health problems, cancer, and coronary heart disease.

It is interesting to note that some recent findings suggest that stress can have an effect on the brain and memory. One report showed that several days of exposure to high levels of the stress hormone cortisol can impair memory.[7]

In his interesting book on the subject, J. Douglas Bremner presented two main theses:[8] (1) Stress-induced brain damage is responsible for a spectrum of trauma-related psychiatric disorders—making these disorders, in effect, the result of neurological damage, and (2) Stressors, acting through a depression of disruption of mental processes, can translate directly into an increased risk for poor health outcomes, including heart disease, cancer, and infectious disease.

Effect of Stress on Children

Unquestionably, stress among adult family members will also have an effect on children in the family. Although not too much is known about long-range effects of childhood stress, one study is of particular interest.[9]

This study examined the etiology of suicidal behavior from cognitive and developmental perspectives in a sample of 181 suicidal and nonsuicidal college students. It was hypothesized that cognitive functioning would serve as a mediator between early life events and suicidal behavior. The study examined child maltreatment, family instability, and poor general family environment as early negative life events, and examined self-esteem, hopelessness, and problem-solving deficits as cognitive factors. In addition, individuals' perceived social support before age eighteen and current social support and life stress were also examined in relation to the preceding variables. Findings indicated that early negative life events have a mild impact on suicidal behavior, but a stronger impact on cognitive deficits, which in turn have a strong impact on suicidal behavior.

In closing this chapter, and at the risk of repeating myself, I want to stress (no pun) the importance of adults having some knowledge about the subject of stress themselves, so that they may help children to better understand it.

Chapter 3

Childhood Emotions

Control yourself! This common expression is very often used in reference to emotional restraint. At one time or another all of us, children and adults alike, demonstrate emotional behavior as well as ordinary behavior. Differences in the individual person and the environment will likely govern the degree to which each individual child expresses emotional behavior.

Adults should not think in terms of always suppressing the emotions of children. On the contrary, the goal should be to help children express their emotions as harmlessly as possible when they do occur so that emotional stability will be maintained. If this can be accomplished the stress resulting from harmful emotional behavior can at least be reduced, if not eliminated entirely.

Emotional stress can be brought about by the stimulus of any of the emotional patterns. For example, the emotional pattern of anger can be stimulated by the thwarting of one's wishes, or a number of cumulative irritations. Response to such stimuli can be either *impulsive* or *inhibited*. An impulsive expression of anger is directed against a person or an object, while the inhibited expressions are kept under some restraint but may be shown in such overt behavior as skin flushing.

Generally speaking, emotional patterns can be placed into the two broad categories of *pleasant* emotions and *unpleasant* emotions. Pleasant emotional patterns include such things as joy, affection, happiness, and love in the broad sense, while included among the unpleasant emotional patterns are anger, sorrow, jealousy, fear, and worry—an imaginary form of fear. The pleasantness or unpleasantness of an emotion seems to be determined by its strength of intensity, by the nature of the situation arousing it, and by the way the child perceives or interprets the situation.

The ancient Greeks identified emotions with certain organs of the body. For example, in general, sorrow was expressed from the heart (a broken heart), jealousy was associated with the liver, hate with the gallbladder, and anger with the spleen. In regard to the latter, we sometimes hear the expression "venting the spleen" on someone. This historical reference is made because in modern times we take into account certain conduits between the emotions and the body by way of the nervous system and the endocrine system. The part of the nervous system principally concerned with the emotions is the *autonomic* nervous system, which controls functions such as heartbeat, blood pressure, and digestion. When a stimulus of any of the emotional patterns occurs, these two systems activate; if the emotional pattern of fear is stimulated, the heartbeat accelerates, breathing is more rapid, and the blood pressure is likely to rise. Energy fuel is discharged into the blood from storage in the liver which causes the blood sugar level to rise. These along with other bodily functions prepare a person to cope with the condition caused by the fear.

Dealing with childhood emotions should imply that sympathetic guidance should be provided in meeting anxieties, joys, and sorrow and that help should be given in developing aspirations and security. To attempt to reach this objective, we might consider emotions from the standpoint of the emotionally maturing child.

For purposes of this discussion, maturity will be considered as a state of *readiness* on the part of the child. The term is most frequently used in connection with age relationships. For example, it may be said that "Johnny is mature for six years of age." Simply stated, *emotional maturity* is the process of acting one's age.

In general, emotional maturity will be achieved through gradual accumulation of mild and pleasant emotions. Emotional *im*maturity indicates that unpleasant emotions have accumulated too rapidly for the child to absorb. One of the important factors in this regard is the process of *adjustment,* which can be described as the process of finding and adopting modes of behavior suitable to the environment, or to changes in the environment.

The child's world involves a sequence of experiences that are characterized by the necessity for him or her to adjust. Consequently, it may be said that "normal behavior" is the result of successful adjustment and abnormal behavior results from unsuccessful adjustment. The degree of adjustment that the child achieves depends upon how adequately he or she is able to satisfy basic needs and fulfill desires within the framework of the environment and the pattern of ways dictated by society.

When stress is induced as a result of the child's not being able to meet his or her needs (basic demands) and satisfy desires (wants and wishes), *conflict* or *frustration* result. Conflict occurs (1) when choices must be made between nearly equally attractive alternatives or (2) when basic emotional forces oppose one another. Frustration occurs when a need is not met. In an emotionally healthy person the degree of frustration is ordinarily in proportion to the intensity of the need or desire; he or she will objectively observe and evaluate the situation to ascertain whether a solution is possible and, if so, what solution would best enable the person to achieve the fulfillment of needs or desires. (Frustration is a major cause of *aggression* which will be discussed in detail later in the chapter.)

Every person has a *zone of tolerance* or limits for emotional stress within which he or she normally operates. If the stress becomes considerably greater than the tolerance level or if the individual has not learned to cope with problems and to try to solve them intelligently, some degree of maladjustment can result.

In order to counteract some of these problems and to be able to pursue a sensible course in helping children become more emotionally mature, certain factors concerned with emotional development of children need to be taken into account.

FACTORS CONCERNING EMOTIONAL DEVELOPMENT

Some of the factors concerned with emotional development of children that need to be considered are (1) characteristics of childhood emotionality, (2) emotional arousals and reactions, and (3) factors that influence emotionality.

Characteristics of Childhood Emotionality

Ordinarily, the emotions of children are not long lasting. A child's emotions may last for a few minutes and then terminate rather abruptly. The child gets it out of his or her system, so to speak, by expressing it outwardly. In contrast, some adult emotions may be long and drawn out. As children get older, expressing the emotions by overt action is encumbered by certain social restraints; socially acceptable behavior at one age level is not necessarily acceptable at another. This may be a reason why some children develop *moods,* which are states of emotion drawn out over a period of time and expressed slowly. Typical moods of childhood may be "sulkiness" due to restraint or anger, being "jumpy" from repressed fear, and becoming "humorous" from controlled joy or happiness.

The emotions of children are likely to be intense. This might be confusing to some adults who do not understand child behavior. They may not be able to see why a child would react rather violently to a situation that to adults might appear insignificant.

The emotions of children are subject to rapid change. A child is capable of shifting rapidly from laughing to crying or from anger to joy. Although the reason for this is not definitely known, it might be that children do not have as much depth of feeling as adults have. In addition, it could be due to children's lack of experience with emotions, as well as their state of intellectual development. We do know that young children have a short attention span that could cause them to change rapidly from one emotion to another.

The emotions of children can appear frequently. As children get older they manage to develop the ability to adjust to situations that previously would have caused an emotional reaction. This is probably due to the child's acquiring more experience with various kinds of emotional situations. Perhaps a child learns through experience what is socially acceptable and what is socially unacceptable. This is particularly true if the child is reprimanded in some way following a violent emotional reaction. For this reason, the child may try to confront situations in ways that do not involve an emotional response.

Children differ in their emotional responses. One child confronted with a situation that instills fear may run away from the immediate environment. Another may hide behind a parent. Still another might just stand there and cry. Children's different reactions to emotional situations are probably due to a host of factors. Included among these may be past experiences with a certain emotional situation, willingness of parents and other adults to help children become independent, and family relationships in general.

Strength of children's emotions are subject to change. At some age levels certain emotions may be weak and later become stronger. Conversely, some children's emotions that were strong may decline. For example, young children may be timid among strangers, but later they see that there is nothing to fear, and the timidity wanes.

Emotional Arousals and Reactions

If we are to understand the emotions of children, we need to take into account those factors of emotional arousal and how children might be expected to react to them. Many different kinds of emotional patterns have been identified. For purposes here I have arbitrarily selected for discussion the emotional states of fear, worry, anger, jealousy, and joy.

Fear

It is not necessarily the arousal itself but rather the way something is presented that determines a fear reaction. For example, if a child is trying to perform a stunt and is told "if you do it that way you will break your neck," a fear response may occur. It is preferable to use a positive approach in dealing with children.

A child may react to fear by withdrawing. Very young children may react by crying or breath holding. Children under three years of age and some older children may use the "ostrich" approach; the child may hide his or her face to get away from the source of the fear. As children get older, these reactions may decrease or cease altogether because of social pressures. For instance, crying may be considered a "sissy" act, especially among boys. (The validity of this thinking is open to question.) One recent report states that crying is now placed solidly within the context of children's normal emotional development.[1]

The term *fear,* from the Old English *fir,* may have been derived originally from the German word *fahr,* meaning danger or peril. In modern times fear is often thought of in terms of anxiety caused by present or impending danger or peril. Fear is generally defined as a normal and specific reaction to a genuine threat that is present at the moment. Anxiety is usually defined as a more generalized reaction to a vague sense of threat in absence of a specific or realistic dangerous object. However, the terms are often used loosely and almost interchangeably. When fearful or anxious, individuals experience unpleasant changes in overt behavior, subjective feelings (including thoughts), and physiological activity.

Fears differ from anxiety in that the former are negative emotional responses to specific situations or objects, such as speaking before a group or receiving an injection, whereas the latter is an emotional state that tends to be prolonged and may be difficult to link to any specific environmental factor. But fears and anxiety are similar in the feelings they arouse; rapid heartbeat, sweating, quivering or faintness, muscular tension, the need to eliminate, and a sense of dread—the fight-or-flight mechanism. Not all people experience all of these signs of fear, but most experience some of them.

Fears are common among children, particularly in early childhood. Examples are fear of dogs, the dark, and going to school. Childhood fears sometimes appear to be unexplainable and children have marked individual differences in susceptibility to fear. However, evidence suggests that children display a definite tendency to learn adults' fears through identification with them or simply observing adults engage in fearful behavior. For example, if during a storm a child observes a parent being fearful, the child is likely to develop a similar fear and fear response pattern. On the other hand, many childhood fears are functions of direct contact or experience with frightening events (e.g., if the child were attacked by a dog). Parental warnings, without the parent necessarily being fearful of such certain objects or events (e.g., "watch out for strangers," "stay away from fires") may also lead to developmental fears in children.

Too often children's fears tend not to be taken seriously by adults because some adults generally hold the belief that children's fears will pass or that they will grow out of them. However, this may not always be the case, and without treatment many fears may be maintained through adulthood.

Worry

Worry might be considered an imaginary form of fear, and it can be a fear not aroused directly from the child's environment. Worry can be aroused by imagining a situation that could possibly arise; a child could worry about not being able to perform well in a certain activity. Since worries are likely to be caused by imaginary rather than real conditions, they are not prevalent among very young children. Perhaps the reason for this is that they have not reached a stage of intellectual development at which they might imagine certain things that could cause worry. Although children will respond to worry in different ways, certain manifestations such as nail biting may be symptomatic of this condition.

Anger

Anger tends to occur more frequently than fear, probably because more conditions incite anger. In addition, some children quickly learn that anger may get attention that otherwise would not be forthcoming. It is likely that as children become older they may show more anger responses than fear responses because they soon see that there is not too much to fear.

Anger is caused by many factors, one of which is interference with movements the child wants to execute. This interference can come from others or by the child's own limitations in ability and physical development.

Because of individual differences in children, anger responses vary. As mentioned previously, these responses are either impulsive or inhibited. In impulsive responses, the child manifests an overt action either toward another person or an object caused by the anger. For instance, a child who collides with a door might take out the anger by kicking or hitting the door. (This childlike behavior is also manifested by some "adults.") Inhibited responses are likely to be kept under control, and as children mature emotionally, they acquire more ability to control their anger.

A mild controversy exists regarding whether one should vent or restrain anger. A recent report suggests that outright expression of anger may not always be the healthiest solution to stress.[2]

Anger and Aggression

Since anger is closely related to aggression, it is important to discuss this aspect of child behavior. Aggression literally means "to attack." It is ordinarily provoked by anger and results in hostile action. Thus, anger is the emotional pattern which can be outwardly demonstrated by aggression.

In recent years a systematic effort ensued to study childhood aggression—its causes, how it is learned, and how it can be controlled. The following is a list of generalizations derived from these findings.

1. *Children rewarded for aggression learn that aggression pays off.* This generalization is concerned with the extent to which an adult uses praise for achievement. The adult must be able to quickly determine whether success was due more to aggressive behavior than skill or ability. The important issue is the extent of aggressive behavior. Certainly an adult should not thwart enthusiasm. It is sometimes difficult to determine whether an act was due to genuine enthusiasm or to undesirable aggressive behavior.

2. *Children involved in constructive activities may be less likely to behave aggressively.* In the school setting this implies that lessons should be well planned so that time is spent on constructive learning activities thus ensuring that worthwhile learning will take place.

3. *Children who have alternative responses readily available are less likely to resort to aggression to get what they want.* This is concerned essentially with adult-child relationships. Although the school environment generally involves group situations, many one-on-one opportunities occur between teacher and child. This situation pertains as well to the home environment if a parent is willing to spend time on one-on-one relationships. This gives an adult a chance to tell the child the kind of behavior that is expected under certain conditions. For example, a child who *asks* for an object such as a ball is more likely to receive cooperation. A child who *grabs* the ball is more likely to provoke aggression in another child. Teaching reinforcement can increase a child's use of nonaggressive solutions for interpersonal problems.

   The adult should be ready to intervene in a potentially aggressive situation before aggression occurs, encouraging children to use nonaggressive methods to solve conflicts. Verbal alternatives can be provided for the children. For example, "I am playing with this now" or "You can ask him to trade with you."

4. *Children imitate behavior they like; they often adopt an adult's behavior.* Some children are more likely to model their behavior

after teachers rather than other adults, sometimes including parents. Many children want to please their teachers and therefore make serious efforts to do so. Of course, it is helpful if a teacher is nonaggressive in his or her own behavior.

5. *Cooperation may be incompatible with aggression.* This could be interpreted to mean that an adult should consistently attend to and reinforce all cooperative behavior. Children consistently reinforced for cooperative behavior are likely to increase cooperative interactions while simultaneously decreasing aggressive behavior.

It is important to point out the difference between *aggressive* behavior and *assertive* behavior. Assertive behavior has received a great deal of attention in recent years, and rightly so. Self-assertiveness should be considered a basic role in one's life. All of us, adults and children, have a need for self-reliance and confidence in our abilities. This need can be met by asserting ourselves in a manner that pursues our personal goals without too much dependence on others. Certainly one can be assertive without being aggressive.

Jealousy

Jealousy usually occurs when a child feels threatened by loss of affection. Many psychologists believe that jealousy is closely related to anger. Jealousy can be devastating in childhood and every effort should be made to avoid it.

Jealousy is concerned with social interaction that involves persons the child likes or has an emotional attachment to. These individuals can be parents, siblings, teachers, and peers. The child may respond in various ways when he or she believes the relationship is threatened. These include (1) being aggressive toward the one of whom the child is jealous or possibly toward others as well, (2) withdrawing from the person whose affections he or she thinks have been lost, and (3) possible development of an "I don't care" attitude.

In some cases children will not exhibit any of these responses. They might try to excel over the person of whom they are jealous or they might tend to try to impress the person whose affections they think have been lost.

Joy

The pleasant emotion of joy is important in maintaining emotional stability. Causes of joy differ from one age level to another and from one child to another at the same age level.

Joy is most commonly expressed by laughing and smiling. Some people respond to joy with a state of relaxation, which has little or no overt manifestation. Nevertheless, it may be noticed when one compares it with body tension caused by unpleasant emotions.

Factors That Influence Emotionality

If we can consider that a child is emotionally fit when his or her emotions are properly controlled and he or she is becoming emotionally mature, then emotional fitness is dependent upon certain factors that influence emotionality in childhood. The following list describes some of these factors.

1. *Fatigue:* Tired children may become irritable; consequently, actions are taken to prevent fatigue such as scheduled rest periods or fruit juice periods. Some studies show hungry children are more prone to outbursts of anger.
2. *Inferior health status:* Temporary poor health, such as colds, tend to make children irritable. Studies show that fewer emotional outbursts occur among healthy children.
3. *Intelligence:* Studies show that, on average, children with low intelligence have less emotional control than children with higher levels of intelligence. A child may be less frustrated if he or she is intelligent enough to figure things out. The reverse could also be true because intelligent children are better able to perceive situations that are likely to arouse emotions.
4. *Social environment:* In a social environment where quarreling and unrest exist, children are predisposed to unpleasant emotional conditions. Likewise, crowded school schedules can cause undue emotional excitation among children.
5. *Family relationships:* A variety of conditions concerned with family relationships can influence childhood emotionality. These include (1) parental neglect, (2) overanxious parents, and (3) overprotective parents.

6. *Aspiration levels:* An emotionally unstable situation can arise if parent expectations exceed a child's ability. In addition, children who have not been made aware of their own limitations may set goals too high and as a result have too many failures and disappointments.

All of these factors can have a negative influence on childhood emotionality and can possibly induce emotional stress. Therefore, efforts should be made to eliminate or control the negative aspects of these factors.

EMOTIONAL NEEDS OF CHILDREN

Identifying specific components of emotional fitness is a difficult matter. Therefore, in the absence of such definitive components, we need to look in other directions in our efforts to help children maintain satisfactory levels of emotional fitness. Emotional maturity and emotional fitness can be expressed in terms of certain emotional characteristics. Children's needs are reflected in these characteristics.

A number of emotional characteristics at the age levels of five through twelve are identified in the following lists. These lists have been developed through a documentary analysis of many sources that have appeared in the literature in recent years. These characteristics suggest the behavior patterns of the so-called "normal" child. This means that if a child does not conform to these characteristics, it should not be concluded that he or she is seriously deviating from the normal. Each child progresses at his or her own rate and much overlapping of the characteristics occurs for each of the age levels.

Emotional Characteristics of Children Ages Five Through Twelve

Five-Year-Old Child

The emotional characteristics of the five-year-old child include the following:

- seldom shows jealousy toward younger siblings;
- usually sees only one way to do something;

- usually sees only one answer to a question;
- would rather begin again than change plans in the middle of an activity;
- may fear being deprived of his or her mother;
- exhibits some definite personality traits;
- is learning to get along better, but still may resort to quarreling and fighting;
- likes to be trusted with errands;
- enjoys performing simple tasks;
- has a desire to please and do what is expected; and
- is developing the ability to sense right and wrong in specific situations.

Six-Year-Old Child

The emotional characteristics of the six-year-old child include the following:

- is restless and may have difficulty making decisions;
- may have an emotional pattern of anger that is difficult to control at times;
- may have behavior patterns that are often explosive and unpredictable;
- is envious of siblings at times and takes pride in siblings at other times;
- is greatly excited by anything new;
- has behavior that is susceptible to shifts in direction;
- is inwardly motivated and outwardly stimulated;
- may be self-assertive; and
- may be dramatic.

Seven-Year-Old Child

The emotional characteristics of the seven-year-old child include the following:

- may allow his or her responses to be conditioned by curiosity and creative desires;
- may find it difficult to take criticism from adults;

- wants to be more independent;
- is reaching for new experiences and trying to relate to the enlarged world;
- is overanxious to reach goals set by parents and teachers;
- is self-critical and sensitive to failure;
- has more controlled emotional patterns of anger; and
- is becoming less impulsive and boisterous in actions than at age six.

Eight-Year-Old Child

The emotional characteristics of the eight-year-old child include the following:

- dislikes taking criticism from adults;
- is able to give and take criticism in his or her own group;
- may develop enemies;
- dislikes being treated as a child;
- has a marked sense of humor;
- has a tendency to blame others;
- is becoming more realistic; and
- wants to find things out for himself or herself.

Nine-Year-Old Child

The emotional characteristics of the nine-year-old child include the following:

- may sometimes be outspoken and critical of adults he or she knows, even if he or she is genuinely fond of them;
- responds best to adults who treat him or her as an individual and approach him or her in an adult way;
- likes recognition for doing a task and responds well to deserved praise;
- is likely to be shy about public recognition but likes private praise;
- is developing loyalty to and sympathy for others;
- does not mind criticism or punishment if it is fair but is indignant if it is unfair; and

- is disdainful of danger to and safety of self, which may be the result of increasing interest in activities involving change.

Ten-Year-Old Child

The emotional characteristics of the ten-year-old child include the following:

- has an increasing tendency to rebel against adult domination;
- is capable of loyalties and hero worship and is able to inspire it in schoolmates;
- can be easily inspired to group loyalties in club organizations;
- likes the sense of solidarity that comes from keeping a group secret as a member of the group;
- has an increasing tendency to show lack of sympathy for and understanding of the opposite sex; and
- is developing increasingly different behavior and interest from those of the opposite sex.

Eleven-Year-Old Child

The emotional characteristics of the eleven-year-old child include the following:

- may tend to withdraw if unskilled in group games and game skills;
- may, if male, be concerned if he feels he is underdeveloped;
- may appear to be indifferent and uncooperative;
- has quickly changing moods;
- wants to grow up, but may be afraid to leave childhood security behind;
- is developing self-direction and a serious attitude toward work;
- needs approval to feel secure; and
- is developing an idea of his or her own importance.

Twelve-Year-Old Child

The emotional characteristics of the twelve-year-old child include the following:

- is developing a truer picture of morality;
- has a clear understanding of real and causal relations;
- is going through the process of sexual maturation, which involves structure and physiological changes and possible perplexing and disturbing emotional problems;
- is learning to either appreciate good grooming or disregard it, and personal appearance may become a source of great conflict;
- may be easily hurt when criticized or made the scapegoat; and
- is prone to maladjustment when there is not a harmonious relationship between child and adult.

It should be obvious that the above emotional characteristics reflect some of the emotional needs of children at the different age levels. These characteristics should be taken into account if we expect success in meeting such needs of children.

GUIDELINES FOR THE EMOTIONAL DEVELOPMENT OF CHILDREN

It is important to set forth some guidelines if adults are to meet with any degree of success in their efforts to aid in the emotional development of children. The reason for this is to assure, at least to some extent, that attempts to attain optimum emotional development will be based more or less on a scientific approach. The guidelines can take the form of valid *concepts of emotional development*. This approach enables us to give serious consideration to what is known about how children grow and develop emotionally. The following list of concepts of emotional development is submitted with this general idea in mind.

1. *An emotional response may be brought about by a goal's being furthered or thwarted.* Adults should make a very serious effort to ensure successful experiences for every child. In the school setting this can be accomplished in part by attempting to provide for individual differences within given school experiences. The school or home setting should be such that each child derives a feeling of personal worth through making some sort of positive contribution.

2. *Self-realization experiences should be constructive.* The opportunity for creative experiences which affords the child a chance for self-realization should be inherent in all of his or her environments. In the school setting teachers might consider consulting with children to see that all school activities are consulting their needs and, as a result, involve constructive experiences.
3. *Emotional responses increase as the development of the child brings greater awareness and the ability to remember the past and to anticipate the future.* Children can be reminded of their past pleasant emotional responses with words of praise. This can encourage children to repeat such responses in future similar situations.
4. *As the child develops, the emotional reactions tend to become less violent and more discriminating.* A well-planned program of school experiences and wholesome home activities should provide release of aggression in a socially acceptable manner.
5. *Emotional reactions tend to increase beyond normal expectancy toward the constructive or destructive reactions on the balance of furthering or hindering experiences of the child.* For some children the confidence they need to be able to face life's problems may occur through physical expression. Therefore, experiences such as active play in the home surroundings and good physical education programs in the schools have tremendous potential to help contribute toward a solid base of total development.
6. *Depending on certain factors, a child's own feelings may be accepted or rejected by the individual.* Children's environmental experiences should make them feel good and have confidence in themselves. Satisfactory self-concept is closely related to body control; experiences related to physical activity can contribute to body control. Therefore, it is important to consider experiences for young children that will provide them with the opportunity for a certain degree of freedom of movement.

OPPORTUNITIES FOR EMOTIONAL DEVELOPMENT IN VARIOUS ENVIRONMENTS

The home, school, camp, and other environments have the potential to provide for emotional stability. The extent to which this actually occurs is dependent primarily on the kind of emotional climate provided by the adult in charge of the environment. For this reason it appears pertinent to examine some of the potential opportunities that exist for emotional development in the child's environments. The following descriptive list is submitted for this purpose. These opportunities will not happen automatically; adults need to work constantly to try to make such conditions a reality.

1. *Release of aggression in a socially acceptable manner:* This appears to be an outstanding way in which school activities such as physical education can help make children more secure and emotionally stable. For example, kicking a ball in a game of kickball or batting a softball can afford a socially acceptable way of releasing aggression. The same can be said of a home environment where parents provide their children with wholesome recreation and active play opportunities.

2. *Inhibition of direct response of unpleasant emotions:* This statement does not necessarily mean that feelings concerned with such unpleasant emotions as fear and anger should be completely restrained. On the contrary, the interpretation should be that such feelings can take place less frequently in a wholesome environment. This means that opportunities should be provided to relieve tension rather than to aggravate it.

3. *Promotion of pleasant emotions:* Perhaps there is too much concern with suppressing unpleasant emotions and not enough attention given to promotion of pleasant ones. The environment should provide a range of activities through which all children can succeed. All children, regardless of ability, should be offered the opportunity for success, at least some of the time.

4. *Recognition of one's abilities and limitations:* It has already been mentioned that a wide range of activities should provide an opportunity for success for all. This should make it easier in the school setting to provide for individual differences of children so that all of them can progress within the limits of their own skill and ability.

5. *Understanding about the ability and achievement of others:* Emphasis can be placed upon the achievements of the group, along with the function of each individual in the group. Team play and group effort is important in most situations.

6. *Being able to make a mistake without being unduly criticized:* In the school setting this requires that the teacher serve as a catalyst who helps children understand the idea of trial and error. Emphasis can be placed on *trying* and that one can learn not only from his or her own mistakes but also from the mistakes of others. The same approach can apply equally well in the home situation.

This discussion includes just a few examples of the numerous opportunities to help provide for emotional development in the child's particular environment. The resourceful and creative adult should be able to greatly expand this list.

EVALUATING INFLUENCES OF THE ENVIRONMENT ON EMOTIONAL DEVELOPMENT

The essential concern here is how an adult can make some sort of valid evaluation of the extent to which the particular environment contributes to emotional development. This means that the adult should make some attempt to assess experiences with reference to whether these experiences are providing for emotional maturity.

One approach would be to refer to the opportunities for emotional development in various environments just discussed. These opportunities have been converted into a rating scale and may be used by an adult to assess the extent to which experiences in the environment provide for emotional development.

1. The experiences provide for release of aggression in a socially acceptable manner.
   4   most of the time
   3   some of the time
   2   occasionally
   1   infrequently
2. The experiences provide for inhibition of direct response of unpleasant emotions.
   4   most of the time
   3   some of the time
   2   occasionally
   1   infrequently

3. The experiences provide for promotion of pleasant emotions.
   4 most of the time
   3 some of the time
   2 occasionally
   1 infrequently
4. The experiences provide for recognition of one's abilities and limitations.
   4 most of the time
   3 some of the time
   2 occasionally
   1 infrequently
5. The experiences provide for an understanding about the ability and achievement of others.
   4 most of the time
   3 some of the time
   2 occasionally
   1 infrequently
6. The experiences provide for being able to make a mistake without being unduly criticized.
   4 most of the time
   3 some of the time
   2 occasionally
   1 infrequently

If one makes these ratings objectively and conscientiously, a reasonably good procedure for evaluation is provided. Ratings can be made periodically to see if positive changes appear to be taking place. Also, they can be made for a single experience, a group of experiences, or for the total of all experiences. This procedure can help to identify the extent to which experiences and/or conditions under which the experiences take place are contributing to emotional development.

ADULT OBSERVATION OF CHILDHOOD EMOTIONS

It is difficult to specify traits that *always* signal poor emotional fitness, as virtually all such traits may be observed in the most normal of people at one time or another. For example, daydreaming is commonly indicated as a symptom of withdrawn behavior; and yet we know that all normal children daydream, and we also know that various factors, such as boredom and emotional stress, commonly lead to increased daydreaming. My own estimate is that, more often than not, children are reprimanded in school for daydreaming, which is unfortunate; when one considers a daydream to be a pleasant reverie of wish fulfillment, it can be seen as a form of meditation whereby the child extricates himself or herself from the cares and worries of the school day.

When observing behavior for evidence of poor emotional development, it is necessary to think in terms of persistent and extreme traits. For example, habitual, rather than occasional, daydreaming may suggest a tendency to withdraw from reality. Similarly, habitual defiance of adult authority, cruelty, or extreme excitability would suggest a need for careful investigation by specialists to discover the cause. Although isolated episodes of these behaviors might deserve noting, they would not necessarily be symptoms of behavior disorders.

The following list includes some behaviors that are sometimes associated with psychological disturbance:

- withdrawal, shyness, seclusiveness, and timidity;
- fearfulness and strong anxiety;
- tenseness, excitability, and lack of emotional control;
- extreme desire to please;
- lack of self-confidence and an "I can't" attitude;
- inability to assume responsibility for one's own errors;
- unhappiness and feelings of depression;
- suspiciousness;
- avoidance of the need to adjust to others;
- inability to adjust to the group, especially at play;
- nail biting, tics, and finger or lip sucking;
- hostile and aggressive behavior;
- destructiveness;
- cruelty;
- temper tantrums;
- irresponsibility;
- showing off and other attention-seeking activities;
- lying, cheating, and stealing;

- preoccupation with sex; and
- failure to make progress that is in keeping with one's physical and mental capacity.

The persistence and severity of these symptoms must, of course, be evaluated in individual cases.

Because so many of the emotional conditions of adulthood have their beginnings in childhood, it is extremely important that adults be alert to emotional deviations in children that may be the insidious beginnings of emotional ill health that will reach its climax in adult life.

Chapter 4

Helping Children Understand Themselves

Children face endless challenges and demands during the development process. It is the responsibility of adults who deal with children to help them adjust to these challenges and demands.

An increasing sentiment exists among many young men and women of high school and college age that they need to *find* themselves. This should fortify the notion that one of the most important aspects of the "growing up" years is that children develop an understanding of themselves. This can be accomplished to some extent when adults improve upon their own knowledge of growing children. Perhaps more important, adults must be prepared to use this knowledge as children grow and develop. This is the major focus of this chapter.

To set the stage for the discussion that will follow, appropriate consideration should be given to *"self*-concerns that induce stress in children." My extensive work with children has enabled me to identify many of the factors that concern them and are stressful for them. The following descriptive list is intended to alert the reader to these concerns and to facilitate an understanding of actions that need to be taken to assist children in understanding themselves.

1. *Self-concerns associated with achieving personal goals:* Stress can result if adults set goals for children that are too difficult for them to accomplish. For example, goals may be much higher than a particular home or school environment will permit children to achieve. On the contrary, when goals are set too low, children may develop the feeling that they are not doing as much for themselves as they should. This aspect of stress is also concerned with some children's fears that they will not meet their life goals. This can sometimes happen early in a child's life.
2. *Self-concerns that involve self-esteem:* This involves the way a child feels about himself or herself. Self-esteem can often be re-

43

lated to the fulfillment of certain *ego needs.* Some children may feel that not enough opportunities are offered for them to succeed in modern society. This is perhaps more true of those children living in a low socioeconomic environment. In addition, some children are bothered when adults do not praise them for what the children consider a job well done.

3. *Self-concerns related to changing values:* It is frustrating for some children if they do not understand the value system imposed upon them by some adults. They may develop the feeling that adults do not value factors which children believe are important to them personally at their various stages of development.

4. *Self-concerns that center around social standards:* In some cases children become confused with the difference in social standards required at the different levels of development. It is sometimes difficult for them to understand that socially acceptable behavior at one age level is not necessarily appropriate at another age level.

5. *Self-concerns involving personal competence and ability:* This might well be the self-concern that frustrates children the most. Lack of confidence in one's ability can be devastating to the morale of the child. Many children are becoming increasingly concerned with their ability, or lack thereof, to cope with problems such as expectations of parents and keeping up with schoolwork.

6. *Self-concerns about their own traits and characteristics:* Children are concerned about being different from the so-called average or normal child. This involves the social need of *mutuality,* which is their desire to be like their peers. When children deviate radically from others in certain traits and characteristics, it can be a serious stress-inducing factor. A specific example is the child who is extremely overweight. Some child psychiatrists believe that overweight children are likely to mature into overweight adults and are more vulnerable to the emotional stress of being overweight than adults. Some studies show that overweight children may get lower grades in school, that in some cases they may be discriminated against by teachers, and that they often have poor social skills.

All of these self-concerns are not characteristic of all children, particularly because of the individual differences among them. A serious concern for one child may be a minimal concern for another. Nonetheless, these self-concerns can serve as guidelines for adults in some of their dealings with children.

UNDERSTANDING CHILD DEVELOPMENT

Development is concerned with changes in the child's ability to function at an increasingly higher level, as when an infant progresses from creeping to crawling. This is later followed by the developmental stage of walking when the child moves to an upright position and begins to move forward by putting one foot in front of the other.

The several major theories of child development each have devoted followers. My position is that various aspects of each theory are useful to adults who have responsibilities for guiding children through the developmental years. My purpose is to make some generalizations about various theories in an effort to provide useful information for adults to apply in their dealings with children.

Regardless of the theory or combination of theories of child development that one believes in, all children are going to experience some sort of undesirable stress at one time or another. Many children may never have to contend with more than the average amount of stress caused by the growth and developmental process. However, other children may be encumbered with such serious life event stressors as divorce, hospitalization, death in the family, etc.

In general, children are grouped into three classifications in terms of their ability to deal with stress. One group of children seems to cope with stress extremely well. They recover soon and are able to incorporate the stressful experience into their everyday life experience. They have a great deal of confidence in themselves and when they encounter a stressful situation and cope with it successfully, their self-confidence tends to increase. Incidentally, these are the children who are associated with adults who deal well with stress.

Another group of children can cope with stress to some extent but have to work at it. They gain more self-confidence as they improve their ability to cope. However, they do not seem to have as high a level of successes as those classified as "exceptional copers."

The third level of classification involves children who have a great deal of difficulty in coping with stress. They have problems struggling with some of the processes of normal growth and development. In addition, they become upset and disorganized by the daily hassles as well as life-event stressors. As might be expected, this group of children associates with adults—particularly parents—who also have a difficult time adjusting to certain life situations that bring about stress.

The aim of adults, of course, should be to help all children become successful in their dealings with undesirable stress. With some knowledge of child development, adults should be in a better position to provide environments that will help children cope effectively with stress during their developmental years.

Total Development of Children

A great deal of evidence indicates that a human being must be considered as a whole and not a collection of parts. This means that a child is a unified individual—the *whole* child. Adults should aim toward total development in order to adequately meet children's developmental needs.

Total development consists of the sum of the individual's *physical, social, emotional,* and *intellectual* aspects. Thus, these aspects become the major *forms* of development. Other forms of development can be satisfactorily subclassified under these major forms. For example, *motor* development, which is defined as a progressive change in motor performance, is considered to be a part of the aspect of physical development. In addition, *moral* development, which is concerned with the capacity of the individual to distinguish between standards of right and wrong, could be considered as a dimension of the broader aspect of social development. This is to say that moral development involving achievement in the ability to determine right from wrong is influential in the individual's social behavior.

Total development is "one thing" comprising the various major forms of development. All of these components—physical, social, emotional, and intellectual—are highly interrelated and interdependent. All are of importance to well-being. The condition of any one of these forms of development affects other forms to a degree and thus total development as a whole. When a nervous child stutters or becomes nauseated, a mental state is not necessarily causing a physical symptom. On the contrary, a pressure imposed upon the child causes a series of reactions, which include thought, verbalization, digestive processes, and muscular function. The mind does not necessarily cause the body to become upset; the total organism is upset by a particular situation and reflects its upset in several ways, including disturbance in thought, feeling, and bodily processes. The whole child responds in interaction with the social and physical environment, and as the child is affected by the environment, he or she in turn has an effect upon it.

In the foregoing statements, an attempt has been made to indicate rather forcefully that the major forms of development are basic components that achieve total development of the child. However, each of these forms of development has certain specific concerns and as such warrant separate discussions. This appears extremely important if one is to understand the role of each form of development as an integral part of total development. The following discussions of the physical, social, emotional, and intellectual forms of development as they relate to children should be viewed in this general frame of reference.

Physical Development

One point of departure in discussing physical development could be to say that "everybody has a body." Some are short, some are tall, some are lean, and some are fat. Children come in different sizes, but all of them are born with certain capacities that are influenced by the environment.

It might be said of the child that he or she "is" his or her body. It is something that child can see. It is his or her base of operation. The other components of total development—social, emotional, and intellectual—are somewhat vague as far as the child is concerned. Although these are manifested in various ways, children are not always as aware of them as they are of the physical aspect. Consequently, it becomes important that a child learn early in life to gain some degree of control over his or her body, or what can be termed *basic body control*. The ability to do this will vary from one child to another. It will likely depend upon the child's degree of physical fitness. The broad area of physical fitness can be broken down into certain components, and it is important that children achieve to the best of their ability with these components. Although there is not complete agreement on the identification of these components, the general consensus is that they consist of muscular strength, endurance, and power; circulatory-respiratory endurance; agility; speed; flexibility; balance; and coordination. (A more detailed account of this subject will be dealt with in Chapter 8 on "Physical Activity, Exercise, and Stress.")

Social Development

Social development is still quite vague and confusing, particularly where children are concerned. It was a relatively easy matter to identify certain components of physical fitness such as strength, endurance, and the like. However, this does not necessarily hold true for components of social fitness. The components of physical fitness are the same for children as for adults. On the other hand, the components of social fitness for children may be different from the components of social fitness for adults. By some adult standards children might be considered as social misfits because certain behaviors of children might not be socially acceptable to some adults.

To the chagrin of some adults, young children are uninhibited in their social development. In this regard we need to be concerned with social maturity as it pertains to the growing and ever-changing child. We need to give consideration to certain characteristics of social maturity and how well they are dealt with at the different stages of child development. Perhaps adults should ask themselves such questions as: Are we helping children to become more self-reliant by giving them independence at the proper time? Are we helping them to be outgoing and interested in others as well as themselves? Are we helping them to know how to satisfy their own needs in a socially desirable way? Are we helping them to develop a wholesome attitude toward themselves and others?

Emotional Development

In considering the subject of emotion some of the comments made in Chapter 3 will be repeated here for the purpose of continuity. We are confronted with the fact that for many years emotion has been difficult to define, and, in addition, ideas and theories have changed in the study of emotion. The purpose here is not to attempt to go into any great depth on a subject that has been one of the most intricate undertakings of psychology for many years. However, a few general statements relative to the nature of emotion do appear to be in order.

In Chapter 3 emotion was defined as a response an individual makes when confronted with a situation for which one is unprepared or which is interpreted as a possible source of gain or loss. As suggested, there are pleasant emotions and unpleasant emotions. Joy is considered a pleasant emotional experience while fear is an unpleasant one. It is interesting to note that much of the literature is devoted to unpleasant emotions. Books on psychology give much more space to such emotional patterns as fear, hate, and guilt, than to the pleasant emotions of love, sympathy, and contentment.

Generally speaking, the pleasantness or unpleasantness of an emotion seems to be determined by its strength or intensity, by the nature of the situation arousing it, and by the way a child perceives or interprets the situation. The emotions of young children tend to be more intense than those of adults. If adults are not aware of this aspect of child behavior, they will not be likely to understand why a child reacts rather violently to a situation that to them seems somewhat insignificant. The fact that different children will have varied reactions to the same type of situation also should be considered. For example, an event that might anger one child might have a rather passive effect on another.

Intellectual Development

Children possess varying degrees of intelligence, and most fall within a so-called "normal" range. In dealing with this form of development we should perhaps give attention to what might be considered components of intellectual fitness. However, this is difficult to do. Because of the somewhat vague nature of intelligence, it is practically impossible to identify specific components of it. Thus, we need to view intellectual fitness in a somewhat different manner.

For purposes of this discussion, I will consider intellectual fitness from a standpoint of how certain factors influence intelligence. If we know this then we might better understand how to contribute to intellectual fitness by improving upon some of these components. Some of the elements that tend to influence intelligence are (1) health and physical condition, (2) emotional disturbance, (3) certain social and economic conditions, and (4) children under stress. When adults have a realization of these issues perhaps they will be more able to help children achieve their intellectual pursuits.

Stages of Development

In considering the various developmental stages of children, adults should understand that descriptions of such stages reflect the characteristics of the so-called "average" child. Although children are more alike than they are different, even identical twins differ in at least one or more characteristics. Therefore, the reader is reminded that the traits and characteristics included in the following discussion are suggestive of the behavior of the "normal" child. This implies that if a given child does not conform to these characteristics, it should not be implied that he or she is seriously deviating from the norm. Each child progresses at his or her own rate and overlapping will occur from one stage of development to another.

I will consider the first stage of development to be that period from birth to fifteen months. This can be designated as the "intake" stage because behavior and growth is characterized by *taking in*. In addition to food the intake stage encompasses sound, light, and the various forms of total care.

At this stage, *separation anxiety* can occur. Since the child depends upon the mother or other caregivers to meet his or her needs, separation may be perceived as a deprivation of these essentials. It is at this stage that the child's overseer—ordinarily the parent—should try to maintain a proper balance between meeting the child's needs and "overgratification." Many child development specialists seem to agree that children who experience some stress from separation gain the opportunity to organize their psychological resources, which helps them adapt to stress. On the contrary, children who do not have this balance may be those who tend to disorganize under stress. They fall into the previously mentioned third level of classification of children who have a great deal of difficulty coping with stress.

During the stage from about fifteen months to three years children are said to develop autonomy. This can be described as the "I am what I can do" stage. Autonomy develops because at this age most children can now move about rather easily. The child does not need to rely on a caregiver to meet every single need. Autonomy also results from the development of mental processes because the child can think and put language to use.

During this stage the process of toilet training can be a major stressor. Children are not always given the needed opportunity to express autonomy during this process. It can be a difficult time for the child because he or she is ordinarily expected to cooperate with and gain the approval of the principal caregiver. If the child cooperates and uses the toilet, approval is forthcoming; however, some autonomy is lost. If he or she does not cooperate, disapproval might result. Some clinical psychologists believe that if this conflict is not resolved satisfactorily, it will emerge during adulthood in the form of highly anxious and compulsive behaviors.

The next stage, from three to five years, can be described as "I am what I think I am." Body movement skills are being used in a more purposeful way. Children develop the ability to daydream and make believe and these are used to manifest some of their behaviors. Pretending allows them to be what they want to be—anything from alligators to zebras. It is possible, however, that resorting to fantasy may result in stress because some children may become scared of their own fantasies.

The range of age levels from five through seven usually includes children from kindergarten through second grade. During this period the child begins his or her formal education. In U.S. culture the child leaves the home for a part of the day to take his or her place in a classroom with children of approximately the same age. Not only is the child taking an important step toward becoming increasingly more independent and self-reliant, but as learning takes place he or she moves from being a highly self-centered individual to becoming a more socialized member of a group.

This stage is usually characterized by a certain lack of motor coordination because the small muscles of the hands and fingers are not as well developed as the large muscles of the arms and legs. Thus, as the child starts formal education he or she needs to use large crayons or pencils as one means of expression. The urge to action is expressed through movement since the child lives in a movement world so to speak. Children at these age levels thrive on vigorous activity. They develop as they climb, run, jump, skip, or keep time to music. An important physical aspect at this stage is that the eyeball is increasing in size and the eye muscles are developing. This factor is an important determinant in the child's readiness to see and read small print, and, thus, it involves a sequence from large print on charts to primer type used in children's books.

Although the child has a relatively short attention span, he or she is extremely curious about the environment. At this stage adults can capitalize upon the child's urge to learn by providing opportunities for him or her to gain information through firsthand experiences and the use of the five senses. The child sees, hears, smells, feels, and even tastes in order to learn.

The age range from eight to nine years is the stage that usually marks the time spent in the third and fourth grade. The child now has a wider range of interests and a longer attention span. Although strongly individualistic, the child is working more from a position in the group. Organized games should afford opportunities for developing and practicing skills in good leadership and followership as well as body control, strength, and endurance. Small muscles are developing, manipulative skills are increasing, and muscular coordination is improving. The eyes have developed to a point where the child can read more widely. The child is capable of getting information from books, and is beginning to learn more through vicarious experience. However, experiments carry an impact for learning at this stage by appealing to the child's curiosity. This is the stage in the child's development when skills of communication (listening, speaking, reading, and writing) and the number system are needed to deal with situations both in and out of school.

During the ages from ten through twelve most children complete fifth and sixth grades. This is a period of transition for most as they go from childhood into the preadolescent period of their development. They may show concern over bodily changes and are sometimes self-conscious about appearance. At this stage children tend to differ widely in physical maturation and emotional stability. Greater deviations in development can be noted within the sex groups than between them. Rate of physical growth can be rapid, sometimes showing itself in poor posture and restlessness. Some of the more highly organized team games such as softball or modified soccer, and the like help furnish the keen and wholesome competition desired by children in this stage of development. It is essential that adults recognize that, at this stage, prestige among peers is more important than adult approval. During this stage the child is ready for a higher level of intellectual skills, which involve reasoning, discerning fact from opinion, noting cause-and-effect relationships, drawing conclusions, and using various references to locate and compare the validity of information. The child is beginning to show more proficiency of expression through oral and written communication.

Thus, after the child enters school and completes the elementary school years, he or she develops (1) socially, from self-centered individual to a participating member of a group; (2) emotionally, to a higher degree of self-control; (3) physically, from childhood to the brink of adolescence; and (4) intellectually, from learning by firsthand experience to learning from more technical and specialized resources.

MEETING THE NEEDS OF CHILDREN

It was mentioned previously that the main difference between physical stress and psychological stress is that the former involves a real situation, while psychological stress is more concerned with foreseeing or imagining an emergency situation. Many child psychologists believe that undesirable stress is due primarily to the failure of adults to help children meet their needs.

In discussing needs of children it is important that we consider their *interests* as well. Although needs and interests of children are closely related and highly interdependent, certain important differences need to be taken into account.

Needs of children, particularly those of an individual nature, are likely to be innate. On the other hand, interests may be acquired as products of the environment. It is possible that a child may demonstrate an interest in a certain unsafe practice that is obviously not in accord with his or her needs at a certain age level. The two-year-old may be interested in running into the street but this practice could result in injury. Acquiring a particular interest because of environmental conditions is further illustrated in the case of children coming from families that are superstitious about certain kinds of foods or certain foods eaten in combination. In such cases, acquiring such an interest from other family members might build up a lifetime of resistance to a certain kind of food that might be very nutritious and beneficial to the child's physical needs.

One of the most important aspects of child development is that of obtaining a proper balance between needs and interests. However, arriving at a suitable ratio between needs and interests is not an easy task. Although we should undoubtedly think first in terms of the child's needs we must also have his or her interests in mind. A general principle by which we might be guided is that the *lower* the age level of children the more we should take the responsibility for meeting their needs. This is based on the obvious assumption that the younger the child the less experience he or she has had, and, consequently, less opportunity to develop certain interests. In other words, a lack of interest at an early age might possibly be synonymous with ignorance regarding a particular subject or situation.

Classification of Needs

It is a well-known fact that children's needs have been classified in many ways. However, it should be remembered that any classification of human needs is usually an arbitrary one made for a specific purpose. For example, when one speaks of biological needs and psychological needs it should be understood that each of these, although classified separately, is interdependent. The classification of needs used here is the same that we used for the forms of development— physical, social, emotional, and intellectual needs.

Physical Needs

Needs of a physical nature are concerned with the basic anatomical structure and basic physiological function of the human organism. Included here, of course, are the need for food, rest and activity, and proper care of the eyes, ears, teeth, etc. Physical needs are also concerned with strength, endurance, agility, flexibility, and balance, previously considered as elements of physical fitness of the human organism. The physical aspect can be measured most accurately with objective instruments. We can tell how tall or heavy a child is at any stage of development. Moreover, persons trained for the purpose can derive accurate information with measurements of blood pressure, blood counts, urinalysis, and the like.

Social Needs

The importance of social needs is brought more clearly into focus when we consider that human beings do most things together. Social maturity and social fitness might well be expressed in terms of fulfillment of certain needs. In other words, if certain social needs are being adequately met, the child should be in a better position to realize social fitness. Among other needs, we must give consideration to (1) the need for *affection* which involves acceptance and approval by persons; (2) the need for *belonging* which involves acceptance and approval of the group; and (3) the need for *mutuality* which involves cooperation, mutual helpfulness, and group loyalty.

When it comes to evaluating social outcomes we do not have the same kind of objective instruments that are available in computing accurately the physical attributes of children. Primarily for diagnostic purposes, some school systems have successfully used acceptable *sociometric* techniques. However, the social aspect is difficult to appraise objectively because of its vague nature.

Emotional Needs

For many years, ideas and theories have changed as far as the study of emotion is concerned. The degree to which emotional needs are met has considerable influence upon the development of the child's personality and mental health. Among the basic emotional needs are (1) the need for a sense of security and trust; (2) the need for self-identity and self-respect; (3) the need for success, achievement, and recognition; and (4) the need for independence.

The human personality is remarkably adaptive and some children whose basic emotional needs are not met in some way are sometimes able to compensate in ways that still attain satisfactory mental health. For example, some orphan children learn to develop certain personality resources which compensate for what some would consider a lack of security. However, if a child's emotional needs are continually not met, the child can easily develop emotional problems or personality disorders.

Many psychiatrists and psychologists believe that the foundation of mental health problems are laid in early childhood. Thus, it appears that adults play a major role in the development of "good" or "poor" mental health. Clearly, the obligation of adults and particularly parents is great to provide the home conditions which will encourage the basis of good future mental health. All children cannot intellectualize upon or evaluate their basic emotional needs. Most children react instinctively in seeking to meet their needs; thus, many facets of their personalities and patterns of adjustment are being developed unconsciously. This is why most people do not know how they got many of their strong feelings about such issues as jealousy, hostility, sex, or religion, for example. At any rate, how children see themselves, other people, and the world at large, and how they interpret and react to each of these, is molded and colored by their early experience.

When we attempt to evaluate the emotional aspect of children's needs we tend to encounter much the same situation as when we attempt to assess the social aspect. However, the emotional aspect might be more difficult to appraise than the social aspect. Among some of the methods used by researchers to attempt to measure emotional response are blood pressure, blood sugar analysis, pulse rate, and galvanic skin response (a device somewhat like the lie detector apparatus). These methods and others have been used by investigators of human emotion and they have limited degrees of validity. In attempting to assess emotional reactivity, investigators sometimes encounter problems in determining the extent to which they are dealing with a purely physiological response or a purely emotional response. Then, too, the type of emotional pattern is not identified by the measuring device. For example, a *joy* response and an *anger* response could show the same or nearly the same measure in microamperes when using a galvanic skin response device.

Intellectual Needs

Satisfactorily meeting children's intellectual needs is one of our greatest concerns, as it is of paramount importance to success in school and life in general. Generally these intellectual needs include (1) a need for challenging experiences at their own level; (2) a need for intellectually successful and satisfying experiences; (3) a need for the opportunity to solve problems; and (4) a need for the opportunity to participate in creative experiences instead of always having to conform.

Assessment of the intellectual aspect is made by a variety of intelligence quotient (IQ) tests. However, this measurement should not always be used as a valid measure of a child's intellectual ability, and many child psychologists tend to feel that this is more a measure of achievement than it is of basic intelligence. Incidentally, I have found that children who are under stress score 12 to 15 percent lower on intelligence tests than children who are not.

It can be concluded that when adults have a better realization of the physical, social, emotional, and intellectual needs of children, perhaps they can more effectively help them with their life pursuits and help them cope with undesirable psychological stress.

TOWARD A CHILD'S UNDERSTANDING OF SELF

Among the various other struggles a child encounters in the process of growing and developing is that of gaining an understanding of *self*. This section provides information that will help adults become more successful in their efforts to aid children in the self-realization process.

In the beginning of this chapter a comment was made about young men and women being concerned with finding themselves. If adults can assist children throughout the growing years to gain a better understanding of themselves, it will be easier for them to transition into young adulthood.

Adults, and particularly parents, should provide a stable sanctuary which the child knows will be there when needed. Children need to be accepted for themselves, with their own unique abilities and limitations. They need to be permitted to grow and learn at their own rate and in their own way—and not made to feel inadequate in growing and learning, even though they may not conform themselves to some standard or "norm." They need to identify as distinct individuals; and their uniqueness is deserving of respect. As children mature they should have the opportunity to assume independence and responsibilities that are commensurate with their age and abilities.

Children require consistent and reasonable control and discipline. It must be understandable to them. A few clear and simple rules are usually sufficient and tend to give children a feeling of security; they know what they can do and what they cannot do. Therefore, children need defined limits to prevent them from destructive behavior and perhaps from even destroying themselves. Consistency in all aspects of the environment is very important. For example, acts for which they are ignored, praised, or punished should not vary from time to time. If they do, children are likely to become confused and their adjustments will be more difficult. Similarly, expression of love should not be intermittent and the threat of withdrawal of love should not be used as a weapon to control behavior.

Modern standard dictionaries ordinarily list almost 400 hyphenated words beginning with *self*—self-abandonment to self-worth. In this discussion I will be concerned primarily with self-image, or how one perceives oneself or one's role. It was suggested earlier that the child is essentially concerned with the *physical self*. The child can see the body and this is much more meaningful than the social, emotional, and intellectual self. Related to this is the term *body image*. This is the child's conception of his or her bodily person and abilities. It has been clearly demonstrated that when adults help children improve upon body image a basic understanding of the broader aspect of self is likely to be established.

Determining Deficiencies in Body Image

One of the first steps is to determine if a child has problems with body image. It is doubtful if any foolproof method exists for detecting problems of body image in children. Many mannerisms said to be indicative of body-imaging problems can also mimic other deficiencies. Nevertheless, those persons who are likely to deal in some way with children should be alert to certain possibilities of such deficiencies.

Generally speaking, deficiencies concerned with body image can be detected in two ways. First, an adult can observe certain behaviors. Second, some relatively simple diagnostic techniques can be used to determine such deficiencies. The following generalized list contains examples of both of these methods.

1. One technique often used to diagnose possible problems regarding body image is to have children make a drawing of themselves. The primary purpose of this is to see if certain parts of the body are *not* included in the drawing. My own personal ex-

perience as a certified Stanford-Binet intelligence test examiner revealed possibilities for such a diagnosis in the test item involving *picture completion*. In this test item a partial drawing of a man is provided for the child to complete. Since the child's interest in drawing a man dates from his or her earliest attempts to represent things symbolically, it is possible through typical drawings by young children to trace certain characteristic stages of perceptual development. It has also been found that the procedure of drawing a picture of himself or herself assists in helping to detect if there is a poor body image.

2. Sometimes the child with a lack of body image may manifest tenseness in movements. The child also may be unsure of his or her movements when attempting to move the body segments.

3. If the child is instructed to move a body part, such as placing one foot forward, he or she may direct attention to the other body part before making the movement. In other cases, he or she may look at another child to observe the movement before attempting to make the movement.

4. When instructed to move one body part (arm) the child may also move the corresponding body part (other arm) when it is not necessary. For example, the child may be asked to swing the right arm and he or she may also start swinging the left arm simultaneously.

5. In such activities as catching an object, the child may turn toward the object when this is not necessary. For example, when a ball thrown to the child approaches he or she may move forward with either side of the body, rather than trying to catch the ball with the hands while both feet remain stationary.

Improving upon Body Image

In general, it might be said that when a child is given the opportunity to use his or her body freely in enjoyable movement an increase in body image occurs. More specifically, activities can be used to help children identify and understand the use of various body parts as well as the relationship of these parts to one another.

Over several years I have conducted a number of experiments in an attempt to determine the effects of participation in certain body-movement activities on body image. The following is an example of this approach utilizing the game Busy Bee.

Busy Bee

In this game the children are in pairs facing each other and dispersed around the activity area. One child who is the *caller* is in the center of the area. This child makes calls such as "shoulder-to-shoulder," "toe-to-toe," or "hand-to-hand." (In the early stages of the game it might be a good idea for the adult leader to do the calling.) As the calls are made, the paired children go through the appropriate motions with their partners. After a few calls, the caller will shout, "Busy Bee!" This is the signal for every child to get a new partner, including the caller. The child who does not get a partner can name the new caller.

This game has been experimented with in the following manner: As the children played the game, the adult leader made them aware of the location of various parts of the body in order to develop the concept of full body image. Before the game was played, the children were asked to draw a picture of themselves. Many did not know how to begin, and others omitted some of the major limbs in their drawings. After playing Busy Bee, the children were asked again to draw a picture of themselves. This time they were more successful. All of the drawings had bodies, heads, arms, and legs. Some of them had hands, feet, eyes, and ears. A few even had teeth and hair.

The following activities can be used for diagnosis for lack of body image, body-image improvement, evaluation of body-image status, or various combinations of these factors. Some of the activities have existed for many years, and others have been developed for specific conditions. They can be carried out in various environments such as school, camp, or home.

Everybody Goes

All of the children (except the one who is *It*) line up side by side at one end of the activity area. *It* stands in the middle of the activity area facing the line. At the opposite end of the area there is a goal line. The distance of the playing area can vary. The game is started with the following rhyme:

> Head, shoulders, knees, and toes.
> Eyes, ears, mouth, and nose.
> Off and running everybody goes.

On the last word, "goes," the children in the line run to the other end and try to reach the goal line without being tagged *It*. All of those tagged become helpers for *It* and the game continues with the children running to the opposite end on signal. If the game is played in its entirety, it continues until one player is left who can be declared the winner.

As the rhyme is recited, the children in the line do the following motions: Head—place both hands on the head; shoulders—place both hands on the shoulders; knees—bend at the waist and place both hands on the knees; toes—bend down and touch the toes and resume standing position; eyes—point to the eyes; ears—point to the ears; mouth—point to the mouth; nose—point to the nose.

It might be a good idea in the early stages for the adult leader to recite the rhyme. The leader can be the judge of how fast this should be done. The more accomplished the children become, the faster the rhyme can be recited, and the children themselves can recite it in unison. When the game is first played, the leader can observe closely those children who are reacting by doing what the rhyme says. It may be found that some are having difficulty. Thus, the activity becomes a means of diagnosing a poor body image. With practice, children will improve in their response to the rhyme.

Mirrors

One child is selected to be the leader and stands in front of a line of children. This child goes through a variety of different movements and the children in the line try to do exactly the same thing; that is, they act as mirrors. The leader should be changed frequently.

In this activity the children become aware of different body parts and movements as the child in front makes the various movements. The adult leader should be alert to see how well and how quickly the children are able to imitate the movements.

Move Along

The children lie on their backs on the floor. The adult leader gives a signal such as the beat of a drum or clap of the hands and the children move their arms and legs in any way they choose. The leader gives direction to the children, such as, "Move your legs like a bicycle," and then gives the signal to begin the movement. If the leader wishes, some sort of scoring system can be devised to reward those children who make the correct movement in the fastest amount of time.

The leaders should observe closely to see how rapidly the children respond to the movements called. In addition, the leader should observe to see if some children are waiting to see what others are going to do before making the correct movement.

Changing Circles

Several circles are drawn on the floor with one less circle than the number of participants. The one child who does not have a circle can be *It* and stands in the middle of the area. The adult leader calls out signals in the form of body parts. For example, such calls could include, "hands on knees," "hands on head," "right hand on your left foot," and so on. After a time the leader calls out, "Change circles!" whereupon all the children try to get into a different circle while the child who is *It* tries to find a circle. The child who does not find a circle can be *It* or a new person can be chosen to be *It*.

The leader should observe closely to see how the children react to the calls, and whether or not they are looking at the other children for clues. As time goes on and the children become more familiar with body parts, more complicated calls can be made.

Body Tag

In this game one child is selected to be *It*. He or she chases the other children and attempts to tag one of them. If the child who is *It* is successful the child tagged can become *It*. If this child does not succeed within a reasonable amount of time a new *It* can be selected. In order to be officially tagged, a specific part of the body must be tagged by the one who is *It*. Thus, the game could be shoulder tag, arm tag, or leg tag as desired.

The leader observes the child to see whether or not he or she tags the correct body part. To add more interest to the activity, the leader can call out the part of the body to be tagged during each session of the game.

These activities are just a few possibilities for use in improving upon body image and an understanding of self. Creative adults should be able to think of numerous other games or procedures that could satisfy this purpose.

Chapter 5

Stress in the Home
and School Environments

Children between six and twelve years old generally spend nine months of the year primarily at home or at school. It is the purpose of this chapter to examine certain aspects of these two environments which can induce stress in children. Such information will be useful to adults by helping them to become more aware of these factors and assist children in dealing with them.

HOME AND FAMILY STRESS

The magnitude of home and family stress on children is well documented. For example, of the life events that are most stressful for children, well over half of them are concerned with home and family. Changes in society with consequent changes in home conditions likely make child adjustment difficult.

Such issues as changes in standards of female behavior, larger percentages of households with both parents working, economic conditions, and mass media can complicate the life of the modern-day child.

Some psychiatrists are convinced that certain home conditions can have an extremely negative influence on children's personality and mental health, not only at their present stage of growth and development, but in the future as well. In fact, studies show that the interaction of stress factors is especially important. Most of these studies tend to identify the following factors that are strongly associated with childhood (and possibly later) psychiatric disorders:

1. severe marital discord,
2. low social status,
3. overcrowding or large family size,
4. paternal criminality,
5. maternal psychiatric disorder, and
6. admission into the care of local authorities.

If only one of the above conditions is present, a child is no more likely to develop psychiatric problems than any other child. However, when two of the conditions occur, the child's psychiatric risk increases fourfold.

Dimensions of stressful events can be discussed in terms of entrances and exits in life events, affect and stress, and multiple stressors. The theory and research on families and children is drawn from different disciplines, thus making a coherent theory difficult. Much theorizing has been done by family sociologists and family systems psychiatrists who have concentrated on the entire family system while neglecting the individual adaptation. In contrast, the psychological literature has largely dealt with the adaptation of individuals to stress. Psychological studies have dealt with self-reports and direct observation, although there seems to be a renewed interest in old methods—such as parental interviews—being used in new ways. Two notable psychological forces have broadened contemporary perspectives on stress and coping; the life-span movement and the ecological movement. The research suggests that most children can cope and adapt to the short-term crisis, such as divorce, within a few years. However, if the stress is compounded by other stresses and continued adversity, developmental disturbances may occur. Variables such as temperament and personality, developmental status, sex, and support systems modify responses to stress.

The Stress of Child Abuse

The magnitude of child abuse is shown by the fact that the government spends upward of $1 billion annually on this serious problem. In addition, various organizations such as the Child Welfare League of America spend considerable time and money on this horrendous condition.

Obviously, child abuse can be a serious stressor for some children. A review of the research on this subject can be summarized as follows:

1. Social stressors associated with child abuse include unemployment, lack of social support, stressful life events, and high levels of confusion.
2. Sociological and maternal characteristics are inextricably intertwined in mutual causal relationships in child abuse.
3. Early separation during the postpartum period (failure of bond formation) is also associated with maternal abuse and neglect.
4. Both situational stress and strength of social networks are significant predictors of abuse.
5. Mothers living in highly stressful situations who report strong social networks are less likely to be abusers than mothers living in high-stress situations who report weak social networks.
6. Physically and emotionally abusive mothers fail to regulate their behavior in relation to the performance of their children. Such a response style is more likely to occur in the context of situationally induced stress.

Sexual abuse is a very serious form of child abuse. According to a report from the National Institute of Mental Health, childhood abuse can have significant long-term biological consequences and can cause "changes in the brain's stress response system."[1] A seven-year study followed 170 girls ages six to fifteen years, half of whom had been sexually abused. Endocrine- and immune-system function was compared to a control group with no history of such trauma. The abused girls had abnormally high levels of stress hormones, which have been shown to cause damage to brain cells crucial to thinking and mental capabilities. In addition, they also demonstrated higher levels of antibodies associated with impairment of immune-system function.

Divorce and Marital Dissolution

The number of children who have experienced parental divorce has tripled during the past several years. In fact, about half of all marriages end in divorce. Millions of children are living with a divorced parent and one-third of all children have experienced parental divorce during childhood and adolescence.

Children frequently experience depression, anger, self-blame, anxiety, and low self-esteem after divorce. In addition, social interaction problems, noncompliance, aggression, and school difficulties occur more frequently among children of divorce than children from intact families. For some children, divorce produces mild or transient behavior problems, but for many others, this transition in family structure leads to enduring emotional and behavioral difficulties. Various aspects of divorce and stress have been studied and several important results can be identified as follows:

1. Much of the confusion in studying the impact of divorce on children has been a result of failure of adults around them to view divorce as a process involving a series of events and changes in life circumstances, rather than a single event.
2. At different points in this sequence children are confronted with different adaptive tasks and will use different coping strategies.
3. In understanding the child's adjustment to divorce it is important to look not only at changes in family structure but also at changes in family functioning and stresses and support systems in the child's extrafamilial social environment.
4. Personal distress and child-rearing attitudes are rarely influenced by age, number of children, or length of marriage.
5. Some studies indicate that the preschool-aged population is the most vulnerable to divorce, whereas others insist that no differences exist.
6. Children of divorce may exhibit both internalizing problems, such as emotional differences, life sadness, fear and grief, and externalizing problems, such as aggression, lower educational achievement, and increased absenteeism.
7. Divorce has gender-specific impacts. Aggression is more common for boys and increased depression is more often reported in girls.
8. Divorce can have a profound impact on the parent-child relationship, possibly due to lack of social support among family members.

9. The impact of divorce for two-thirds of children is limited to two years, but numerous studies have found a host of long-term effects, such as lesser educational attainment.

Life Changes

Although some children seem to take any kind of change in their lives in stride, many others tend to suffer serious distress as a result of it. Often, these life changes can cause certain psychological consequences.

One study conducted several years ago involved family relocation and examined the effects that moving and separation have on families. The authors suggested a role for mental health agencies in easing these stressful life events.[2] These studies include variables such as knowledge of family separation, father's entry and reentry into the family, and mobility in general. Families that experience heightened alienation experience greater problems. Children whose fathers are frequently absent are reported to experience greater dependency needs and more academic problems and to have higher referral rates for emotional problems. Literature on stress in the corporate family closely parallels findings on military families. A move consists of four stages: (1) preparation, (2) migration, (3) overcompensation, and (4) decompensation. Approaches used to strengthen family functioning during relocation include (1) education, (2) competency promotion, (3) community organization, and (4) natural caregiving. Four methods of corporation assistance are recommended. These include the establishment of relocation officers to oversee operations, a site visit by family, educational seminars for employees and spouses, and publications about moving. It was concluded that community care and information can ease the stress of moving families and help them cope with new circumstances.

Sibling Stress

The fear that some children have of the prospect of being replaced by or at the least, "taking a back seat to" a new arrival can be stress inducing. Since the average American family has two-plus children, most families at one time deal with this issue. Some researchers have attempted to shed light on problems that can occur when a new baby enters the family. The following summary of findings seems warranted:

1. During the first month postbirth mothers are sometimes viewed as less warm, supportive, and protective toward the firstborn. They also may be less consistent when disciplining the child.
2. Firstborns sometimes show an increase in sleep and eating problems and poor physical health.
3. Negative behavior in the social-emotional area increases, especially with females.
4. The mother's awareness of potential difficulties of the availability of outside assistance to the family, the reaction of the firstborn, the mother's physical health, and the father's behavior in relation to the mother and firstborn all appear to influence stressfulness.
5. Three months postbirth, changes in the behavior of parents and firstborns are in a generally positive direction.
6. Six months postbirth, mothers experience highest levels of personal stress and conflict in the marital relationship. Physical ill health on the part of the firstborn seems to be a major problem at this time.
7. The reduction of stress within the family following the birth of a child is viewed as an important goal for families to try to attain.

SCHOOL STRESS

A number of conditions exist in many school situations that can cause much stress for children. These conditions prevail at all levels—possibly in different ways—from the time a child enters school until graduation from college. The child or adolescent who is facing a set of demands with insufficient resources may respond in many ways that are harmful or maladaptive.

Miscoping responses can include behavioral and environmental responses such as social withdrawal, alcohol or drug abuse, and truancy. In the cognitive area, an imbalance of demands and resources could result in feelings of low self-esteem and beliefs about being a failure. Related to these is the possible evolution of "learned helplessness," the belief that one's actions essentially are unrelated to the consequences experienced.

Stress and the Child in the Educational Process

School anxiety as a child stressor is a phenomenon with which educators, particularly teachers and counselors, frequently find themselves confronted. Various theories have been advanced to explain this phenomenon and relate it to other character traits and emotional dispositions. Literature on the subject reveals the following characteristics of anxiety as a stress-inducing factor in the educational process:

1. Anxiety is considered a learnable reaction that has the properties of a response, a cue of danger, and a drive.
2. Anxiety is internalized fear aroused by the memory of painful past experiences associated with punishment for the gratification of an impulse.
3. Anxiety in the classroom interferes with learning, and whatever can be done to reduce it should serve as a spur to learning.
4. Test anxiety is a near universal experience, especially in this country, which is a test-giving and test-conscious culture.
5. Evidence from clinical studies points clearly and consistently to the disruptive and distracting power of anxiety effects over most kinds of thinking.

It would seem that causes of anxiety change with age, as do perceptions of stressful situations. Care should be taken in assessing the total life space of the child (background, home life, school life, age, sex) in order to minimize the anxiety experienced in the school. It seems obvious that school anxiety, although manifested in the school environment, may often be caused by unrelated factors outside the school.

The Stressfulness of School Adjustment

One of the most stressful life events for some young children is beginning the first grade. One of the reasons for this may possibly be that older childhood friends, siblings, and even some unthinking parents admonish the child with, "wait until you get to school—you're going to get it." This kind of negative attitude is likely to increase any separation anxiety the child already has.

It was mentioned previously that separation anxiety begins in the first stage of a child's development, from birth to fifteen months. It can reach a peak at the latter part of the developmental stage from three to five years, because it is the first attempt to become a part of the outer world—entering school. For many children this is the first task of enforced separation. For those who do not have a well-developed sense of continuity, the separation might be easily equated with the loss of the life-sustaining mother. The stress associated with such a disaster could be overwhelming for such a child. Learning to tolerate the stress of separation is one of the central concerns of preschoolers; adults should be alert to signs and seek to lessen the impact. Compromises should be worked out, not necessarily to remove the stress, but to help the child gradually build a tolerance for separation.

In extreme cases of the separation problem, a child's reaction typically may include temper tantrums, crying, screaming, and downright refusal to go to school. Or, in some instances, suspiciously sudden aches and pains might serve to keep the "sick" child home. What the child is reacting against is not the school, but separation from the mother. The child might perceive the stress associated with this event as a devastating loss equated with being abandoned. The child's behavior in dealing with the stress can be so extreme as to demand special treatment on the part of the significant adults in his or her life.

The aim in such cases always should be to ease the transition into school. It is important to keep in mind that the separation is a two-way street. Assuring parents of the competence of the school staff and the physical safety of their child may go a long way toward helping lessen the stress. If adults act responsibly and with consistency, the child should be able to make an adequate adjustment to this daily separation from family and, in the process, learn an important lesson in meeting reality demands.

Stress and Competition in the School Environment

In a study conducted with 200 fifth- and sixth-grade children one of the questions I asked was, "What is the one thing that worries you most in school?" Responses were various, however, the one general characteristic that tended to emerge was the emphasis placed on *competition* in so many school situations. Although students did not state this specifically, the nature of their responses clearly indicated this concern.

Most of the literature on competition for children has focused on sports activities; however, many situations in classrooms can cause stress. An example is the spelling bee, which still exists in some schools and, in fact, continues to be recognized in an annual national competition. To say the least, failing at any school task in front of others can be embarrassing.

It is interesting to note that the terms *cooperation* and *competition* are antonymous; therefore, the reconciliation of children's competitive needs and cooperative needs is not an easy matter. In a sense, we are confronted with an ambivalent condition which, if not carefully handled, could place children in a state of conflict, thus causing them to suffer distress.

In generalizing on the basis of my own experience and examination of the available evidence with regard to the subject of competition, it seems justifiable to formulate the following concepts:

1. Very young children in general are not extremely competitive, but become more so as they grow older.
2. A wide variety of competition is evident among children; some are violently competitive, while others are mildly competitive, and still others are not competitive at all.
3. In general, boys tend to be more competitive than girls.
4. Competition should be adjusted so there is not a preponderant number of winners over losers.
5. Competition and rivalry produce results in effort and speed of accomplishment.

Those who deal with children at the various educational levels might be guided by these concepts. Competition should not necessarily be restrained. On the other hand, it should be kept under control, so that competitive needs of children are met in a satisfactory and wholesome manner.

How the 3Rs Can Stress Children

Various school subjects could be considered stressful for many children. Prominent among school subjects that have a reputation for being more stress inducing than others are the basic "3Rs" (reading, writing, and arithmetic). Attending school daily and performing poorly is a source of considerable and prolonged stress for many children.

If children overreact to environmental stresses in terms of increased muscular tension, this may interfere easily with the fluid movement required in handwriting tasks, decreasing their performance and further increasing environmental stresses. Many educators have seen children squeeze pencils tightly, press hard on the paper, purse their lips, and tighten their bodies, using an inordinate amount of energy and concentration to write although still performing at a very low level.

Reading is another school activity loaded with potential anxiety, stress, and frustration for many children. One of the levels of reading recognized by reading specialists is called the "frustration level." In behavioral observation terms, this can be described as the level in which children evidence tension, excessive or erratic body movements, nervousness, and distraction. This frustration level is said to be a sign of emotional tension or stress with breakdowns in fluency and a significant increase in reading errors.

The subject that seems to stress the greatest majority of students is mathematics. This condition prevails from the study of arithmetic on entering school through the required courses in mathematics in college. Mathematics has become such a problem in recent years that an area of study called "math anxiety" is receiving increased attention.

One source defines math anxiety as "feelings of tension and anxiety that interfere with the manipulation of numbers and the solving of mathematical problems in a wide variety of ordinary life and academic situations."[3] This same source suggests that causes of math anxiety may include unpreparedness, school absenteeism, parents perpetuating the myth that mathematics ability is hereditary, and negative past experiences with teachers.

As a result of stressful experiences in school mathematics classes, "math-anxious" and "math-avoiding" people have developed; these individuals tend not to trust their problem-solving abilities and experience a high level of stress when asked to use them.

Teachers who make an effort to reduce the number of stressful situations in mathematics programs will be helping their students to become better mathematics learners as well as helping them become more confident and capable performers in mathematics tasks as adults. The same could be said for reading and writing tasks.

The Stress of School Tests

In more than forty years as a teacher—which included all levels from elementary school through the university graduate level—I have observed many students who were seriously stressed by "testphobia," or what has now become known more commonly as *test anxiety.*

Perceived stress appears to depend on psychological sets and responses that individuals are more likely to bring to the testing situation than to manufacture on the spot. Students respond to tests and testing situations with learned patterns of stress reactivity. The patterns may vary among individuals and may reflect differences in autonomic nervous system conditioning, feelings of threat or worry regarding the symbolic meaning of the test or test-taking situation, and coping skills that govern the management of complexity, frustration, information load, symbolic manipulation, and mobilization of resources. Individual patterns occur of maladaptive behavior such as anxiety, as sustained level of autonomic activity after exposure to a stressor, and the use of a variety of such defense mechanisms as learned helplessness and avoidance behavior.

Perceived stress also depends upon the nature of the task to be performed. As tasks get more complex and require greater degrees of coordination and integration of the nervous system, a given stressor level will affect task performance as if it were a stronger stressor.

What then, does the nature of test anxiety imply for educational goals and practice? Perhaps continuing opportunities should be provided for all school personnel and parents to report on their experiences with the tests that have been used. This feedback should also place a great deal of emphasis on the students' reactions to their testing experiences. The reactions of children that give evidence to emotional disturbance in relation to tests should be carefully considered, especially when test results are interpreted and used for instructional, guidance, and administrative purposes.

Finally, it is important to take a positive attitude when considering test results. That is, emphasis should be placed on the number of answers that were correct. For example, the child will be more likely to be encouraged if you say, "You got seven right," rather than, "You missed three." This approach can help minimize stress in future test taking.

Chapter 6

Stress and the Child with an Affliction

Many labels have been applied to children who deviate somewhat from the so-called "normal" child. Perhaps the most common label used in the past is the term *handicapped*. In its purely literal meaning, a handicap is a disadvantage that makes achievement unusually difficult. I prefer the more recently used term *challenged* because it best characterizes the categories of children that will be dealt with in this chapter.

The categories of challenge as they are concerned with stress that will be discussed in this chapter are: (1) disease, (2) developmental disabilities, (3) slow learning, and (4) psychic trauma. These categories have been selected arbitrarily. They are not necessarily listed in order of importance, and in some instances overlapping may occur from one category to another.

STRESS AND CHILDREN WITH DISEASE

In an extensive literature review on stress and disease, disease was not found to be quite as difficult a concept as stress. Some of the literature can be summarized as follows.

Similar to stress, disease has quantitative and temporal aspects which hinder its investigation. Pathology takes time to develop. In some cases it takes many years, showing few if any signs or symptoms until the disorder has progressed quite far. With slowly progressive disorders it may be difficult to decide in a nonarbitrary way when an individual has the disease. If the early stages are subtle enough, it may be difficult even to conceptualize what it means to have the disease. For instance, has a person had cancer when a microscopic but progressing malignancy has been eliminated by host defenses?

The furtiveness of pathology is one of the reasons why choosing disease measures for research can be troublesome. The best measures are usually objective indexes of pathology, but they may not exist or be too costly to employ. Less definitive measures such as self-reports of diseases or symptoms and utilization of health care services are often used. However, it is well known that reports of symptoms and visits to physicians need not reflect actual medical pathology. Also, as more publicity is given to the idea that stress affects disease, more potential research subjects are likely to look for and report symptoms or to seek medical attention when they perceive themselves to be under stress. Psychological distress may confound disease outcome measures.

In summary, both stress and disease are rather slippery terms. The point to be kept in mind is that every conceptual operation or semantic confusion about variables tends to obscure their relationships. If we are not certain when disease has occurred and we are not sure what stress is, we can expect difficulty in determining how they are related.

Pelletier[1] once reported a tragic consequence, that stress-related psychological and physiological disorders have become the number one social and health problem and further, that most standard textbooks attribute anywhere from 50 to 80 percent of all disease to stress-related origins. Selye went so far as to say that stress is involved in *all* diseases, indicating that every disease causes a certain amount of stress, since it imposes demands for adaptation upon the body.[2] In turn, stress plays some role in the development of every disease; its effects—for better or for worse—are added to the specific changes characteristic of the disease in question.

One of the most important findings has produced evidence linking stress and the body's ability to fight disease. Some studies suggest the possibility of immune-system malfunction under stress by comparing the infection-fighting capability of white blood cells taken from normal and severely stressed individuals. In the case of children this becomes more serious, because generally they have weaker immune systems than adults.

At one time or another most children acquire some sort of disease and in the past some of the less serious ones have been labeled "childhood diseases." If properly cared for, most children will survive such diseases with little or no long-term effects. More of a concern are the more serious acute and/or chronic diseases and the stress they cause for the child and his or her family members. Some representative research reports follow.

Piening studied the effect of illness-related stress on the emotional life and interactions of families of renal diabetes patients.[3] Case examples, primarily of young to middle-aged diabetics, were used to illustrate family stress situations and the guilt and blame often assumed by parents of diabetic children. It was noted that professionals who work with renal diabetic patients must be aware that the stress any particular family feels depends on the family's structure, pre-existing family mental health, and the effect of diabetes on family life.

Hollander and Florin conducted a study with fourteen asthmatic nine- to eleven-year-olds and fourteen controls matched for age, social class, and sibling constellation who were exposed to a stress-inducing competitive achievement situation.[4] Facial expression of emotions were systematically analyzed from video recordings, and peak expiratory flow rate (PEFR) reduction was measured from pre- to poststress. Asthmatics showed a significantly lower frequency and duration of overall emotional expression than their controls. Specifically, the frequency and duration of expressed anger/rage, enjoyment/joy, and surprise/startle were lower in asthmatics. Moreover, duration of overall expressed emotion showed a significant negative correlation with PEFR reduction in the asthmatic group, indicating a relevant relationship between facial expression of emotions and breathing function.

Barbarin and Chesler studied families of children with cancer to investigate the relationship between parental coping strategies and stress, marital quality, relations with medical staff, and relationships with friends and neighbors.[5] Fifty-five families consented to the interview and questionnaire; the data in this report were provided solely by parents of surviving children. The ages of the children with cancer ranged from four to twenty-one years at the time of the interview. With the exception of one black family, all families were white. Mothers (n = 42) ranged in age between twenty-eight and fifty-seven years. Thirty-three percent of the participating families had children with leukemias, 19 percent with lymphomas, 18 percent with brain and central nervous system (CNS) cancers, 12 percent with osteogenic sarcomas, 11 percent with Wilms' tumor, and 7 percent with other cancers. The following coping strategies were assessed: information seeking, problem solving, help seeking, maintaining emotional balance, relying on religion, being optimistic, denying, and accepting. Results showed a stronger association between coping and the quality of relationships with medical staff than any of the other psychological outcomes assessed.

STRESS AND CHILDREN WITH DEVELOPMENTAL DISABILITIES

Developmental disabilities can be considered as defects that prevail or limit a child from participating in those activities for his or her age group. Such disabilities may be caused by a disease or an accident or they may be the result of a birth defect. Some developmental disabilities are readily apparent, such as blindness; others may be "hidden," as in the case of a heart problem.

The child with a developmental disability, through no fault of his or her own, can sometimes be a problem for parents and other family members. Parents in particular must be acutely aware of the disabled child's needs and how to meet them as well as they can. On the other hand, siblings should not suffer neglect as a result of one family member having a developmental disability. In many instances, regardless of family members' efforts to deal positively with a child with a developmental disability, stress can take its toll on everyone involved.

Gallagher, Beckman, and Cross[6] did a research review on sources of stress and its amelioration in families with developmentally disabled children. They wanted to find out about the stresses families experience and the support factors necessary to help them with their disabled children. They found that stress appears to increase with the child's age. Other general factors affecting stress included low family income, divorce, and separation. The father often plays a limited role in these families, even when present. Both formal and informal social support networks are important to these families, often more so than professional support, which has been uneven. Families must be treated as having individual needs that require individual solutions, as should their children. Investigators and practitioners are encouraged to continue their focus on the family as a legitimate unit of study and treatment as far as family stress is concerned.

Wikler, Haack, and Intagliata[7] examined issues faced by divorced mothers of developmentally disabled children and found that stressful circumstances of these mothers are greater than those of either divorced mothers of "normal" children or married mothers of disabled children. Stresses of divorced mothers of developmentally disabled children included child care, financial, social stigmatized identity, emotional, and lack-of-information issues. It was noted that the extra caregiving demands, combined with the lack of social responsiveness and temperament problems in the disabled child, correlated with increased stress for the single mother. Family interventions for single mothers of developmentally disabled children included family support services, family network therapy, family therapy, and group therapy. Group work was found to be a useful, efficient, and effective family intervention. A parent can participate in a specialized parent group while receiving family support services, family network therapy, and family therapy. These various interventions are compatible and they do not duplicate one another in their impact. Since long-term planning and support are advocated for these clients, these services could be offered sequentially and strategically over time.

In a study involving deaf children, Greenberg[8] studied the effects of early intervention for families of such children. He presented findings on an independent evaluation of an early intervention program for profoundly deaf children. The comprehensive intervention program served twelve families with children under three years old. The evaluation included comparison to a matched sample of children without intervention. Included were a developmental assessment and assessment of family (Questionnaire on Resources and Stress), knowledge, and functions. Results indicated more developmentally mature communication, lower stress, and higher-quality interaction in families who had received intervention.

STRESS AND SLOW LEARNERS

Along with agreement that the needs of children with learning impairment must be reflected in appropriate teaching techniques, there is an increasing awareness of the problem of identification. Too many children in our classrooms have been mistaken for slow learners because of their difficulty in mastering such basic academic skills as reading and mathematics. It is essential, therefore, to establish a clear understanding of the basic differences between children with the *slow learner syndrome* and those whose learning problems may be caused by factors other than subnormal intellectual functioning.

Generally speaking, those who have problems with learning can be classified in three ways: (1) children with mental retardation; (2) children with depressed potential; and (3) children with learning disabilities.

In the literature, the broad generic term *challenged* encompasses all degrees of mental deficit. The designation of the term *slow learner* has been given to those children who have a mild degree (along a continuum) of subnormal intellectual functioning, as measured by intelligence tests. The intelligence quotients of these children fall within the range of seventy or seventy-five to ninety. These children make average or below-average progress in academic skills, depending upon where they fall along the continuum of mental retardation. Children will probably demonstrate slowness in such academic skills as reading and mathematics. They will very likely have difficulty in the areas of more complex mental processing of defining, analyzing, and comparing. They tend to be poor reasoners. However, these children may not necessarily be equally slow in all aspects of behavior. They may be above average in social adaptability or artistic endeavors.

As far as children with *depressed potential* are concerned, for some years it has been recognized that factors other than intellectual subnormality affect achievement in the classroom. Concern in our schools today for the disadvantaged and culturally different children places increased emphasis on understanding these factors. In considering the term slow learner we need to differentiate between the limited educational achievement of the *constitutional* slow learner and the subnormal intellectual capacity of the *functional* slow learner. The latter are often mistaken by teachers for slow learners with limited potential because they are not achieving in the classroom. These children may be making limited progress in acquiring skills or may have behavior problems. But limited achievements are caused by numerous other factors that serve to depress an individual's ability to learn. Such factors may be the lack of psychological stimulation from limited socioeconomic environment, inadequate hearing and vision, emotional problems with family and peers, malnutrition, or poor general health. It is important to recognize that the situation is not permanent. Both educational programs and conditions affecting the child's physical, psychological, or social well-being can be improved.

In the third classification are children with *learning disabilities,* who do not belong in the categories of the constitutional or functional slow learner, but whose classroom achievements may be similar.

There is an imperative need for proper identification of these children. Often children with learning disabilities are labeled slow or lazy when in reality they are neither. These labels have an adverse effect on future learning, on self-perception, and on feelings of personal worth. Obviously, any of these conditions can be stressful to children.

The research identifying learning-disabled children indicates that their learning has been impaired both in specific areas of verbal and/or nonverbal learning, but their *potential* for learning is categorized as normal or above. Thus, these children fall within the ninety and above IQ range and, in the case of the gifted child, inordinately higher, in either the verbal or nonverbal areas. Total IQ is not used as the criterion for determining learning potential because adequate intelligence (either verbal or nonverbal) may be obscured when the total IQ falls below ninety, but when specific aspects of intelligence fall within the definition of adequate intelligence. In the case of the learning-disabled child whose IQ falls below the normal range, a multiple involvement is considered to be present.

Regardless of the degree of mental deficit or learning disability, most children with any of these problems can be considered stress-prone. The embarrassment and frustration accompanying slow learning can be devastating to some children and to their family members as well.

In studying stress and mentally retarded children, Crnic, Friedrich, and Greenberg[9] indicated that research concerned with families of mentally retarded children has often yielded inconsistent and, at times, contradictory findings. This inconsistency is partly due to methodological inadequacies and a narrow focus on unidimensional variables with unimodal measurements. No succinct model has been presented to explain family adaptation and the range of possible outcomes. The authors present a critical review that focuses on parents, siblings, parent-child interactions, and family systems. A comprehensive conceptual model is proposed that accounts for (1) the range of possible familial adaptations, both positive and negative, involving the impact of perceived stress associated with the presence of a mentally retarded child, and (2) the family's coping resources and ecological environments as interactive systems that serve to mediate the family's response to stress.

Studying the impact of a mentally handicapped child on the family, Seshadri[10] administered a variety of intelligence measures and parental attitude scales to thirty mentally retarded children and their mothers, respectively. Education of the mother was found to be significantly related to her attitudes toward her child. No trends in marital adjustment or parental attitudes were observed. Most mothers perceived that a mentally retarded child was a burden that varied from being moderately to severely troublesome. The greater the degree of the child's retardation, the greater was the perceived burden on the mother.

STRESS RESULTING FROM PSYCHIC TRAUMA

For purposes of this discussion, *psychic trauma* means a psychic behavioral state resulting from emotional stress and/or physical injury. Such states can range from witnessing or being involved in a tragedy within the home and/or family to those of a more massive scale, such as the September 11, 2001, terrorist attacks.

Klingman[11] investigated the effect of primary prevention of stress resulting from mass inoculation in a community. He assessed the effectiveness of a brief, situation-specific, group-administered preparatory intervention in a nonclient school population undergoing mass inoculation against rubella. Fifty-one sixth-grade girls were randomly assigned to practice, no-practice, or control groups. Both practice and no-practice groups received information that described the inoculation procedure and how to cope with it by using cognitive-behavioral coping skills. The practice group was encouraged to perform coping techniques of this type, whereas the no-practice group was told only that the intervention would help them during the inoculation. The controls received only technical information about the inoculation procedure. All subjects completed the State-Trait Anxiety Inventory for Children (STAIC) before and after the intervention. Results indicated that children in both practice and no-practice groups reported less anxiety and exhibited more cooperative behavior during the inoculation than children in the control group, and those who were guided and prompted to actively practice derived greater benefit.

The effects of lightning-strike disaster were investigated by Dollinger, O'Donnell, and Staley.[12] They administered a fear survey to twenty-nine ten- to thirteen-year-old children and their mothers who had been participants or observers when lightning struck a soccer game with a force that knocked down most of the participants and observers and led to the death of one participant.

Two control children were matched to each lightning strike (LS)-child for age and sex, making a total of fifty-eight controls. In addition, measures of children's sleep disturbances and somatic complaints were obtained from their mothers, and the interviewer rated each LS-child for the extent of emotional upset caused by the disaster. Results showed that differences between the LS and control groups were most pronounced for child-reported fears. The generalization gradient was fairly consistent with expectations from classical conditioning theory. The correspondence between mothers' and children's reports of intense storm-related fears was markedly larger in the LS-children than in the controls. Child-reported fears showed a number of substantial relations with mother-reported sleep and somatic problems and with interviewer-rated emotional upset.

Ordway[13] studied the acute and chronic phases of stress following a major residential fire. The investigator, her husband (both practicing psychiatrists), and children were informed that their home had been struck by lightning while they were out of town. No deaths, injuries, or uprooting from the community occurred, since within two and one-half weeks the family was living in a trailer on the property. Nevertheless they suffered disorganization, disorientation, denial, intrusions, grieving, and psychosomatic symptoms. Symptoms of distress, disorganization, and depression were greatest (1) when the news of the fire was received and the visual and olfactory results of the fire were experienced; (2) during the two months the roof was being rebuilt (because of weather damage to the remains); (3) during the third month after the fire; and (4) eleven months after the fire, when the details were being completed. This family still experienced fire-related problems for as long as fifteen months after the event.

The fact that medical hospitalization can be stressful to children is shown in the research of Bassin, Wolfe, and Thier.[14] Research on the impact of medical hospitalization (HZ) on children suggests that there are specific psychological reactions to HZ hinder children's adaptation to the new environment. This research argues that some children do not respond well to the medical regimen because of the psychological stresses inherent in the HZ itself. An awareness and consideration of the emotional factors in HZ are believed to facilitate ill children's acceptance of treatment and subsequently contribute to recovery. This study investigated twelve eight- to thirteen-year-old African-American and Mexican-American psychiatric patients' reactions to their psychiatric HZ, using the children's artwork and storytelling as a database to generate hypotheses. It was predicted that these children would experience reactions similar to their medically hospitalized counterparts. Despite individual differences and unique variations in the data, systematic consistencies supported the prediction. Repetitive themes of separation anxiety, punishment and guilt, and institutional transference were found in both the drawings and descriptive verbalizations of the children. These data were used to generate concomitant coping reactions.

Burgess[15] studied rape trauma syndrome through research involving exploitation of children via sex rings and pornography. She studied forty-nine male and seventeen female six- to sixteen-year-olds who had been exploited by adults. Results of interviews indicated that 75 percent of the children demonstrated patterns of negative psychological and social adjustment after the rings were exposed. More than 61 percent of the children had been ring members for more than a year and slightly more than half of the children had been used in pornographic photographs. A follow-up found four response patterns to stress based on the overt behavioral adjustment of the children: integration of the event, avoidance of the event, repetition of symptoms, and identification with the exploiter. Children who integrated the exploitation were those who had spent the least amount of time in the sex ring and who were least likely to have been involved in pornography.

Again, the reader is reminded that the studies reported in this chapter do not necessarily reflect the total picture. They do, however, provide some representative examples of research regarding stress and children with afflictions.

Chapter 7

Nutrition, Diet, and Stress

Eighteenth-century gastronomist Anthelme Brillat-Savarin, famous for his book *The Physiology of Taste* (1825), once proclaimed, "Tell me what you eat and I will tell you what you are." The modern adage "You are what you eat" could well have been derived from this old quotation. And, of course, it is true. This old saying has been brought more clearly into focus in modern times, as researchers now know that our bodies synthesize food substances known as *neurotransmitters*. Many prominent nutritionists believe these neurotransmitters relay messages to the brain that, in turn, affect our moods, sex drives, appetites, and even personalities. Adding a certain food or omitting another could be just what a person might need.

Related to the issue of diet and stress is what is commonly known as "stress eating." Dr. Gary Small[1] suggests that nearly everyone has experienced some form of stress eating and that the phenomenon generally has two components: (1) a stressful event to trigger binge eating and (2) conveniently available foods, often processed foods or desserts.

At one time eating was fun and enjoyable; however, in recent years, many of us have become victims of the "don't eat this, don't eat that" syndrome. Because certain aspects of nutrition and diet have become so controversial, many people are confused about the entire matter. This chapter will attempt to clear up some of this confusion. Any consideration of the nutrition problems, eating habits, and dietary concerns of both children and adults should be undertaken, if possible, under the guidance and supervision of a physician and/or a qualified nutritionist.

NUTRITION

Nutrition can be described as the sum of the processes by which a person takes in and uses food substances; nutrition is the nourishment of the body by food. The processes involved are ingestion, digestion, absorption, and assimilation.

Ingestion derives from the Latin word *ingestus,* meaning "to take in," and in this context it means taking in food, or the act of eating. The process of *digestion* involves the breaking down or conversion of food into substances that can be *absorbed* through the lining of the intestinal tract into the blood and used in the body. *Assimilation* is the incorporation or conversion of nutrients into protoplasm, which is the essential material making up living cells.

Because the body's needs change as it grows and develops, good nutrition for children is not the same as for adults. In addition to the nutrients needed to sustain present status, children also need certain nutrients to help form new tissues. In her classic book on nutrition, Jane Brody[2] estimates that a five-year-old child weighing forty-four pounds needs as much iron, calcium, and magnesium and even more vitamin D than a twenty-five-year-old man who weighs 154 pounds. Although total quantities are smaller, pound for pound a five-year-old needs twice as much protein, thiamin, riboflavin, niacin, and vitamins A and C, and three times as much B_6 and B_{12} as a twenty-five-year-old man. This does not mean that a young child should be eating as much food as an adult; rather, it means that the calories a child consumes need to be more densely packed with nutrients.

Growing children need plenty of certain minerals to build strong bones and teeth and protein for firm muscles, as well as for energy and stamina. Poorly nourished children will not be likely to grow properly. Thus, it is appalling that possibly more than five million children in the United States experience hunger every month. This is an atrocious record for a country that is the so-called "land of plenty."

Essential Nutrients and Their Functions in the Body

The body needs many nutrients or foods to keep it functioning properly. These nutrients fall into the broad groups of proteins, carbohydrates, fats, minerals, vitamins, and water. (Although water is not a nutrient in the strictest sense of the word, it must be included here, because of its need in the digestive process.) The calorie, which is often mistakenly thought of as a nutrient, is also discussed in this section.

Three major functions of nutrients are: (1) building and repairing all body tissues; (2) regulating all body functions; and (3) providing fuel for the body's energy needs. Although all of the nutrients can function best when they are combined with other nutrients, each still has its own vital role to play.

Protein

Protein is the protoplasmic matter from which all living animal cells and tissues are formed. It is the source of nitrogen, and it is from nitrogen that the building blocks of protein are formed. These basic substances are called amino acids, and they are found in plant and animal food sources.

The amino acids are acted upon and released during the digestive process, absorbed, and then rebuilt into new protein forms. For example, when a protein-rich food such as meat is eaten, the digestive process promptly breaks it down into various amino acids. The body chemistry then goes to work to reassemble these amino acids into new protein form. Some amino-acid combinations form the various hormones of the endocrine system, and still others are used to form enzymes. Enzymes are internal secretions necessary for the proper functioning of the blood, stomach, and other organs of the body. They are highly specialized and are responsible for such varied functions as aiding in the clotting of the blood and turning starches into sugar.

Some of the amino acids are used to make the brain chemicals or the previously mentioned neurotransmitters. Three brain chemicals are dopamine, norepinephrine, and serotonin. An amino acid called tyrosine is important in the making of dopamine, norepinephrine, and tryptophan, an amino acid widely distributed in proteins. Dopamine and norepinephrine are thought to be involved in increased muscle activity, aggressive behavior, and emotional states.

Protein is the basic raw material necessary for growth from the beginning of life. It is necessary for the building of new tissue and repairing worn-out tissue. It can also serve as a fuel for muscular work when needed, and we never outgrow our need for it. Since the metabolic process of the body is continuous, it is imperative that one has a continual supply of protein so the functions of the body can be successfully accomplished.

A body in the process of building itself—that of a growing child—needs a greater proportion of protein to weight than one that has reached its growth potential and uses protein only to repair worn-out tissues. An average adult may require a gram of protein per kilogram of body weight daily, while a growing child may need two to three times this amount.

One source of protein for children is milk, and many nutritionists recommend that a child drink a quart of milk daily. To be sure, for a growing child, milk is an important source of protein, in addition to calcium and vitamin D. However, some children do not like milk, possibly because it is often forced upon them as "the perfect food." In addition, some children are allergic to milk and may lose their ability to digest it. Also, there could be a risk of some children getting too much milk. As milk is not a good source of iron, drinking too much of it (and neglecting other foods) can cause an iron deficiency and predispose a child to anemia.

Although most Americans obtain their protein from both plant and animal sources, certain religious groups, vegetarians, and people living in countries in which producing meat is not economically feasible have demonstrated that various plants provide many of the amino acids that are needed by humans. Plants have the ability to synthesize all of the amino acids that they need for growth, but humans are not self-sufficient. There are at least eight out of the more than twenty-five amino acids necessary to our health and growth that we are incapable of synthesizing satisfactorily from other foodstuffs. The amino acids that the body tissues cannot manufacture and that must be obtained from outside sources are called essential amino acids.

So-called complete protein foods are those that contain all of the essential amino acids. Animal meats are complete in this sense, as are milk, milk products, and eggs. Fish, too, is a good source of complete proteins. On the other hand, large segments of the world's population eat little or no meat and, in some cases no dairy products—but such people still grow into active adulthood. Thus, it is clear that some vegetable foods likely provide all the necessary proteins. Grain foods, nuts, peanuts, soybeans, peas, beans, and yeast are among the more important sources of nonanimal protein. Combinations of proteins seem to be especially valuable for meeting the body's needs.

Although proteins are essential for life and are needed regularly, their importance should not lead to their being exaggerated in the diet. They are especially important when bodily tissues are being rebuilt following a debilitating illness. In other words, the comments concerning the necessity of a continuous supply of proteins, or any other food, should not lead one to think that he or she could not stand to miss an occasional meal, or several meals for that matter. After all, consuming three meals a day is more a conditioned response than a nutritional necessity. (This is particularly important as far as children are concerned, as most of them need more than the three traditional meals daily.) It seems likely that the quality of one's food intake over a period of time—say several days—is more important than a meal-by-meal evaluation. However, nutritionists have made efforts to provide guidance as to what, in general, the body needs daily.

Carbohydrates

The carbohydrates that occur in our foods chiefly as sugar and starches are combinations of the chemical elements of carbon, hydrogen, and oxygen. These foods are broken down during the digestive process into simple sugars, which are then absorbed into the blood. It is from the blood that the tissue cells can withdraw sugar according to their energy needs.

Our main source of carbohydrates is food composed of grains, including breads and cereals (some of which are also rich in protein, minerals, and vitamins), pasta, pastries, and the like. Potatoes also are a source of starch, but they contain other important food values as well.

Another important function of carbohydrates is the provision of fiber (once generally referred to as roughage), which adds bulk and helps to move the bowels. In recent years the lack of fiber in the diet has been of some concern because, on average, adults consume only about 40 percent of the fiber that is necessary. Some children may consume even less.

Generally speaking, usable carbohydrates have at least two roles in the body. The first is the formation of glucose. Glucose is the major energy source for the body and the form of energy used by the brain, nerves, and lung tissue. One gram of carbohydrate yields four calories of energy. The second role of carbohydrates is the formation of glycogen from glucose. Glycogen is a form of stored energy, with the principal stores being the liver. Smaller reserves are found in the muscles. Blood glucose comes from dietary complex carbohydrates and simple carbohydrates. Incidentally, recent guidelines issued by the National Academy of Sciences (NAS) for the first time recommended daily intake for carbohydrates. Children and adults need a minimum of 130 grams daily of carbohydrates to provide enough glucose to the brain.

Fats

Fats are derived from the same chemical elements as carbohydrates, but the proportions of carbon, hydrogen, and oxygen are different. Fats contain more carbon but less oxygen than carbohydrates do, and they are a more concentrated energy source than either carbohydrates or proteins. They also contribute to bodily functioning in other important ways and should not, therefore, be completely eliminated from the diet.

Fat deposits in the body serve as insulation and shock-absorption material and as reserve energy in storage. An individual whose energy expenditure exceeds the energy provided by his or her carbohydrate intake is especially in need of the slow-burning fats in the diet. One who wishes or needs to lose weight or who has certain circulatory disorders and risks is usually advised to restrict fat intake. For several decades, fat has made up about 40 percent of the average diet. Because of the relationship of fat intake to heart disease in adults, it is generally recommended that the fat in the diet not exceed 30 percent. Recent studies have found that children consume far too much fat; this may be due to an excessive intake of junk foods. Incidentally, the new NAS guidelines suggest that a healthy diet can include from 20 to 35 percent calories from fat.

People on a low-fat diet sometimes wonder if they are not getting enough fat. Although this is possible, it is not likely. For example, low-fat foods such as chicken and fish contain some fat. Sometimes strict dieters may even avoid these foods because of their fat content. When one eliminates all animal protein and dairy foods, the diet may be too low in protein, iron, zinc, calcium, and other nutrients. A low-fat diet is not necessarily a no-fat diet. A diet containing 20 percent of calories from fat is considered a low-fat diet.

Fats are classified in two ways: saturated and unsaturated. Some sources of saturated fats are meat fat, whole milk, butter, and cheese. With the exception of fat from milk, some children will not have a great deal of fat in their diets. On the other hand, they might have an overabundance of carbohydrates due to the "sweet-tooth" syndrome. Sources of unsaturated fats are most cooking oils and margarine, although recently margarine has become suspect. It is ordinarily recommended that unsaturated fats be used in preference to saturated fats. In fact, the new NAS guidelines emphasize the use of healthful fat sources such as milk, nuts, olives, soybeans, and corn oil.

Minerals

The mineral elements of the body are often referred to as ash constituents, for they are the residue left from the oxidation of the organic compounds that we eat in the form of food. In simpler terms, we may liken minerals to the ashes that remain after the burning of wood or coal. The mineral elements make up about 4 percent of the total body weight, with calcium accounting for approximately half of the 4 percent.

Included among the minerals are calcium, phosphorus, potassium, sulfur, chlorine, sodium, magnesium, iron, iodine, manganese, copper, cobalt, nickel, and fluorine. Most of the minerals are needed in minute quantities and are plentiful in a good diet. However, calcium, iron, and iodine are needed in appreciable quantities and, therefore, may require special consideration in the diet. As previously mentioned, some children may be heavy milk drinkers and therefore may suffer from a shortage of iron. According to some nutritionists, adults with iron deficiency are not able to work as hard as they normally would, and children may have decreased attention span and decreased learning ability, which disappear when proper levels of iron are returned.

Some studies suggest that children who boost their calcium intake develop significantly greater bone density. However true this may be, adults are cautioned that children may face potential risks from taking calcium supplements. Side effects such as stomach distress and constipation might occur in children. Parents who are considering a calcium supplement for their children should do so under the supervision of a pediatrician or qualified nutritionist.

Since calcium accounts for approximately one-half of the body weight in minerals, it should receive special consideration in this discussion. Although it is one of the very important minerals in the diet, many persons, particularly women, tend to consume one-half of the needed calcium.

Calcium is the basis for strong bones and teeth, with bones containing 99 percent of the body calcium and blood the other 1 percent. Blood calcium is very important because it assists with proper heartbeat, contractions of muscles, and blood clotting.

The major function of minerals in the body is to serve as building and regulatory substances. As structural constituents, they operate in three general ways: (1) they give rigidity to the hard tissues of the bones and teeth; (2) they serve as components of soft tissues in muscles and nerves; and (3) they often serve as the crucial elements in the production of hormones (for example, iodine produces thyroxine). As regulators of body processes, minerals serve in many ways. They (calcium in particular) are essential for the coagulation of blood; protect against the accumulation of too much acid or alkali in the blood and body tissues; are involved in the maintenance of the normal rhythms of the heartbeat; aid in the exchange of water in the tissues; and are involved in the transmission of nerve impulses.

Minerals have important and diverse uses in human metabolism. Since many of them are required in carbohydrate, fat, and protein metabolism, they are important in the energy reaction required during the stress response. However, it is important to take minerals in balanced proportions and not in excessive amounts, since they can be toxic in high doses.

Some people like their food well-seasoned with salt and they sometimes wonder why they are cautioned to use less of it. Salt is made up of sodium (40 percent) and chloride (60 percent). Sodium is important to the body because it helps maintain balance between body fluids and cells. It is also important for transmission of nerve impulses and muscular relaxation.

The U.S. Reference Daily Intakes (RDIs) recommend not more than 2,000 milligrams of sodium per day. Unfortunately, most individuals consume a great deal more than this—sometimes as much as 7,000 milligrams per day. Because high sodium intake is associated with high blood pressure and abnormal fluid retention, persons with high blood pressure and other types of heart disease are ordinarily cautioned by their physician to reduce salt intake. Alternative forms of food seasoning are herbs and spices such as garlic powder, dill, basil, and thyme.

Vitamins

The realization that vitamins are basic nutrients serves as a milestone in the emergence of the field of nutrition as a scientifically based discipline. Unlike such nutrients as proteins, fats, and carbohydrates, vitamins do not become part of the structure of the body; rather, they serve as catalysts that make possible various chemical reactions within the body. These reactions involve converting food substances into the elements needed for use by the body's various cells. For example, vitamin D needs to be present if calcium is to be metabolized and made available for use in the blood and bones.

Water

By far the greatest proportion of the body weight of human beings is water. This liquid, evaporating and flowing from the surface of the body and breathed out as vapor, must be continually replenished for one to remain alive. The chemical changes that make life possible can take place only in solution, and water provides the necessary solvent.

The body gets water from fluids taken as drink, from foods that are eaten, and from the combustion of foods in the body. The body loses water in the form of urine from the kidneys, fecal discharge from the intestinal tract, perspiration from the skin, and exhaled breath from the lungs.

Physical activity, environmental heat, and the daily bodily processes lead to water loss. If this loss is not balanced by water intake, dehydration can occur. For short periods, this loss is harmless and leads to thirst and restoration of normal water level and body weight through copious drinking. However, if the dehydrated state continues over an extended period of time, bodily functions become seriously jeopardized since water is involved in all of them.

A question that often arises is: How many glasses of water should one consume daily? First, it is important to consider that water intake does not involve merely water alone; fruits and vegetables, as well as other liquids, contain water. Physicians are likely to vary in their recommendations about the amount of water one should drink daily. Some will recommend that one start and end the day with an eight-ounce glass of water and consume the same amount at each meal. Others suggest six to eight glasses of water per day.

Many such arbitrary recommendations concerning the desirable water intake per day have been made. However, so many factors affect the need for water—such as the fluid content of food, how active a person is, and the environmental temperature—that one could be inclined to recommend thirst as a guide.

Calories

A common misconception is that a calorie is a nutrient just as fats, carbohydrates, or proteins are nutrients. Actually, a calorie is a unit of measurement, like an ounce or an inch. The body requires energy to function, and heat is the by-product of this energy. A calorie is the amount of heat necessary to raise the temperature of one kilogram (2.2 pounds) of water one degree centigrade. Since food is our source of fuel, scientists have been interested in computing the number of calories that different foods provide, as well as the number of calories that the body must use in the performance of various activities. The results of these studies have furnished information that tells us how many calories or heat units of food we must produce in order to have enough energy to meet our needs. These energy needs may be divided into two categories: voluntary and involuntary. Voluntary activities are those over which we have control, while the involuntary energy demands are those that take place continually, whether we are awake or asleep. Involuntary activities include digestion, heart function, elimination, breathing, and special demands automatically brought on by factors such as emotional excitation, stress, and environmental heat.

Many people are trained from infancy to be especially fond of candies and dessert foods, since these are used by some parents as a reward for cleaning one's plate, eating unwanted foods, and being good in other ways. In excess of bodily needs, the calories from such foods have been called empty calories, because they provide little or no nutritional value. Indeed, they contribute to obesity while at the same time satisfying the appetite when other food values are needed. It is not suggested that an effort be made to eliminate pastries and candies from the diet entirely, but an effort should be made to reduce their prominence. After all, fruits, vegetables, and juices can be equally satisfying foods (if prepared correctly) that are relatively low in calories and high in other nutrients, and they do not confront the body with the problem of disposing of pure, unneeded energy.

A one-year-old child consumes about 1,000 calories daily. By the age of three this rises to 1,300, and by age six increases to 1,700. (Consumption of excessive empty calories can elevate these amounts appreciably.) For the average adult male, the amount of calories consumed is 2,700, and for the average adult female, 2,100.

One way to assess your calorie needs is: If you are completely sedentary, multiply your weight by ten; that is, if you weigh 150 pounds you would probably need 1,500 calories daily. If you are fairly active multiply your weight by twelve or thirteen, and if you are extremely active multiply your weight by fifteen. Incidentally, the new NAS guidelines recommend that the number of calories consumed should be tied directly to how much physical activity one gets.

Digestion

The digestive system of the body is more than thirty feet long from beginning to end, and the chemical processes that occur within the walls of this mucus-lined hollow tube are extremely complex. From the moment that food is taken into the mouth until waste products are excreted, the body's chemical laboratory is at work. The principal part of this system is the alimentary canal, which consists of the oral cavity, pharynx, esophagus, stomach, small intestine, and large intestine. Two additional organs, the liver and the pancreas, are necessary to complete the digestive system. Both connect to the small intestine. It is from these two organs that many of the essential digestive juices are secreted.

As mentioned previously, the function of the digestive system is to change the composition of foods that we ingest. Reduced to simpler chemical substances, the foods can be readily absorbed through the lining of the intestines for distribution by the circulatory system to the millions of body cells. These end products of digestion take the form of simple sugars, fatty acids, minerals, and vitamins.

Digestion is also accomplished by mechanical action. First, the food is broken down by the grinding action of the teeth. (How many times as a child were you admonished to "chew your food and don't gulp it down"?) This chewing increases tremendously the food surface area upon which the various digestive juices can act. The food is then swallowed and eventually is moved through the alimentary canal by a process called *peristalsis,* which is a series of muscular contractions that mix the contents of the digestive tract and move them onward.

Some people have trouble digesting milk due to *lactose intolerance.* This means that the enzyme lactate may be decreasing. This enzyme is needed to break down lactose, a form of sugar found in milk. One may wish to use a substitute for regular milk such as buttermilk, soy milk, yogurt, or cheese. Some use a product called Lactaid, a lactose-free milk.

Digestion and Stress

Sometimes a child's complaint of "bellyache" can be traced to a stressful experience. This is commonly known as *nervous indigestion.* In this regard, the digestive tract is exceedingly responsive to one's emotional state. Food eaten under happy conditions tends to be readily digested. On the contrary, digestion may be impeded and even stopped for a considerable period of time (as much as a day or more) when combined with severe emotional stress. Extensive nervous connections in the digestive tract tend to make its organs especially susceptible to disorders caused by stress. Examples of disorders caused by stress are nausea, diarrhea, and colitis (inflammation of the large bowel). In such disorders the organs involved may not necessarily be diseased and there may only be an impaired functioning of the organ. However, many authorities agree that prolonged emotional stress can lead to serious diseases of the digestive tract. Donald Morse and Robert Pollack[3] contend that stress is the principal reason for digestive disturbance. In their work on stress and saliva it was found that stress causes dry mouth. This is particularly important since digestion starts in the mouth and saliva is needed to start the digestion of starch.

DIET

Diet is an all-inclusive term used to refer to foods and liquids regularly consumed. The question of what constitutes a balanced diet is often raised. A balanced diet includes, along with sufficient fluids, foods from the four basic food groups: the dairy group, the meat group, the vegetable and fruit group, and the bread and cereal group.

A general recommendation is that children receive daily three servings from the dairy group, two servings from the meat group, four or more servings from the fruit and vegetable group, and four or more servings from the bread and cereal group. Recommendations regarding the size of a serving vary but, generally speaking, a child's serving should be one tablespoon for each year of age. For example, a six-year-old child should receive six tablespoons for a serving. The emphasis is not so much on following an arbitrary diet, but on knowing on which foods and proportions of foods one functions best.

Studies by the National Cancer Institute and U.S. Department of Agriculture have found that only about 1 percent of young people meet all of the federal recommendations for the daily consumption of foods from the four basic groups. Sixteen percent do not meet the requirement of any food group. Such studies suggest the need to emphasize low-fat, low-added-sugar options when helping children make food choices; for example, one can encourage consumption of fruits, vegetables, and grains.

Some families' diets include too many potentially harmful foods—cholesterol, for example. Excessive amounts of this chemical component of animal oils and fats can be deposited in the blood vessels and are a factor in hardening of the arteries, which leads to heart attacks.

Cholesterol has become one of the recent health buzzwords. The significance of cholesterol as a risk factor prompted the First National Cholesterol Conference held November 9 through 11, 1988, in Arlington, Virginia. This meeting was sponsored by the National Cholesterol Education Program coordinating committee, which included approximately twenty-five member organizations. This conference was unique in that the researchers, physicians, and policy and program experts shared knowledge and program successes in the rapidly changing field of cholesterol study.

The universal interest in this risk factor is certainly justified by the following statistics:

- More than 50 percent of Americans have cholesterol levels that are too high.
- Only about 8 percent of Americans know their cholesterol levels.

- As many as 250,000 lives could be saved each year if citizens were tested and took action to reduce their cholesterol levels.
- For every 1 percent a person lowers his or her cholesterol level, the risk of heart attack is reduced by 2 percent.
- If your cholesterol is 265 (meaning 265 milligrams of total cholesterol per deciliter of blood) or higher, you have four times the risk of a heart attack as someone with a cholesterol level of nineteen or lower.
- Nine out of ten people can substantially reduce their cholesterol by changing their diets.

Physicians vary widely in their beliefs about acceptable levels of cholesterol, and just a few years ago a broad range of 150 to 300 was considered normal. However, thoughts on this matter have changed radically. For example, the National Heart, Lung, and Blood Institute has announced stringent guidelines. It is now believed that the total blood cholesterol level should not exceed 200.

The National Cholesterol Education Program suggests the following cholesterol levels for children as compared to adults.

Recommended Cholesterol Levels

	Children (mg/dl)	Adults (mg/dl)
Acceptable	less than 170	less than 200
Borderline	170-199	200-239
High	above 200	above 240

Diet and Stress

Most writers on the subject of stress emphasize the importance of diet as a general health measure. However, the following question arises: Are there any specific forms of diet that can contribute to the prevention of stress and/or help us cope with it? In this regard, J. Daniel Palm[4] once developed the theory that many stress-initiated disorders are related to problems that originate in the regulation of the blood-sugar level. This theory, developed as an extension of the data derived from controlled research, states that an insufficiency of sugar in the blood supplied to the brain is enough of a detrimental condition, and therefore a stress, to initiate physiological responses and behavioral changes that develop into a variety of disorders. A deficiency of blood sugar, which is known to be associated with a variety of disorders, is seen not as a consequence of the disease but a primary and original physiological stress. Behavioral changes may be inadequate or inappropriate attempts of the stress-affected person to compensate. It is believed that if the stress of insufficient blood sugar can be prevented, various kinds of abnormal behavior can be controlled. A dietary program was proposed to eliminate this stress. This diet was based on the metabolic characteristics of *fructose* (fruit sugar) and its advantageous use when exchanged for glucose or other carbohydrates, which are digested to glucose and then absorbed. (Fructose itself is a normal constituent of sucrose, which is ordinary table sugar; it also occurs naturally in many fruits and constitutes half the content of honey.)

The previously mentioned Morse and Pollack cautioned that an excess of fructose can also be a problem. This occurs more from the ingestion of soft drinks and processed foods in which the concentration of fructose is often higher than in fruits and juices. It also has been found that when fructose intake is raised to about 20 percent of a person's daily diet (up from the average of 10 to 12 percent), total cholesterol may increase by more than 11 percent and triglycerides are elevated slightly above 56 percent.

CHILDREN'S EATING HABITS

Adult supervision, especially that of parents, is of utmost importance to children's eating habits. Unfortunately, a parent may be the child's worst enemy in this respect. The nagging parent who tries to force upon the child foods that he or she may not like often can do a great deal of harm to the child's present and future eating habits.

At about the end of the first year of life, the eating habits of children undergo remarkable changes. For one thing, a large decrease in the intake of food usually occurs. Many parents do not understand the process of child development and they worry needlessly about this decrease. What actually happens is that, after the first year, the child's growth rate declines and, as a consequence, his or her need for calories per pound of body weight decreases. This causes the appetite to decrease and this can vary from one meal to another, sometimes depending on the kind and amount of activity in which the child engages. A parent who is aware of this will not expect the child of two or three years of age to eat the way he or she did at six months. Parents should be more concerned with the quality of the child's food intake than with the quantity.

Sometimes a child may develop a sudden like or dislike for certain foods. For example, the child may want a particular cereal because of a prize in the box and then may turn the food down because he or she is disenchanted and does not like the prize. Fortunately, more often than not, such likes and dislikes do not last long, and adults should not worry too much about them.

Providing a large variety of foods early in the child's life is a good practice. This helps to prevent a child from forming set likes and dislikes. An adult should set an example by not allowing his or her own dislikes to influence children.

Parents often complain that a particular child is a poor eater. Identifying the cause of poor eating habits is important. It may be that the child too frequently eats alone and is deprived of the pleasant company of others. Perhaps the portions are too large, which can be overwhelming, particularly if the child feels that he or she must consume all of it. Mealtime should be a happy time; it is not a time for reprimanding and threatening if a child does not eat heartily. Such behavior on the part of adults can place the child under stress and create an eating problem that otherwise would not occur.

Some of my own studies of nine- to ten-year-old children have found that children are aware of foods that are best and worst for health. Those foods identified as best for health were vegetables (36 percent), fruits (28 percent), meat (26 percent), bread (8 percent), and milk (only 2 percent, somewhat surprisingly). As for the worst foods for health, 65 percent of the children chose candy and other sweets, 17 percent chose junk foods, 9 percent chose salt, 5 percent chose coffee, and 4 percent chose fats. (This might well be an indication of health knowledge and not necessarily health practice.)

CHILDHOOD OBESITY

On an ABC television news broadcast on November 26, 2002, the announcer commented that eight children in New York (one boy weighing 400 pounds) were suing a McDonald's restaurant for causing their obesity. The complaint was made on the basis of the restaurant failing to provide any health-risk information with the meals. Although critics proclaimed the suit to be frivolous, others wondered if it could be a sign of the times.

Obesity is due to excess storage of fat in the body. It is a serious hazard and can cause such disorders as diabetes and heart disease. For children, these health problems may be years away, but the psychological effects of obesity can be devastating. The obese child may develop negative feelings and loss of self-esteem and personal worth.

Obesity in children has tripled in the past two decades. Kelly Brownell, Director of the Center for Eating and Weight Disorders at Yale University, and David Ludwig of Harvard University believe that the obesity epidemic has many causes, but deterioration in the diet almost certainly plays a role. Fast food is served in massive proportions and contains highly processed carbohydrates and the worst fats, and has little or no fiber. Each of these factors has been linked to increased risk for obesity.[5]

Obesity greatly increases the chance for developing diabetes. It has been reported that people who develop adult-onset diabetes as children (a condition for which prevalence is rising rapidly) can experience severe and occasionally fatal complications. This can begin when people are still in their twenties.[6]

Although some cases of obesity are caused by a glandular condition, most are the result of overeating. Stated simply, obesity results when more calories are ingested than are necessary for energy and the excess food is stored in the body as fat.

Many prominent nutritionists proclaim that obesity is genetic. In families with both parents of normal weight, a child has a chance of only 7 percent of being overweight. If one parent is overweight, the chance of the child being overweight leaps to 40 percent. When both parents are obese, there is an 80 percent chance that the child also will be obese. This suggests a strong hereditary tendency toward obesity, but it does not necessarily prove it. The family environment—especially the parents' eating and exercise habits—is another factor to be considered. In fact, although heredity was once considered of major importance in predicting a person's potential for obesity, the role that it plays is not entirely clear.

Chapter 8

Physical Activity, Exercise, and Stress

When used in connection with the human organism, the term *physical* means a concern for the body and its needs. The term *activity* derives from the word "active," one meaning of which is the requirement of action. Thus, when the two words physical and activity are used together, the term implies body action. This is a broad term and could include any voluntary and/or involuntary body movement. When such body movement is practiced for the purpose of developing and maintaining *physical fitness,* it is ordinarily referred to as *physical exercise*. This chapter discusses both the broad area of physical activity and the more specific area of physical exercise, and takes into account how these factors are concerned with health and how they relate to stress.

THE PHYSICAL ASPECT OF PERSONALITY

One way to begin discussing the physical aspect of personality could be to state that everybody has a body. Some are short, some are tall, some are lean, and some are fat. Children come in different sizes, but all of them have a certain innate capacity that is influenced by the environment.

As far as human beings are concerned—from early childhood through adulthood—it might be said that the body is our base of operation, what could be called our "physical base." The other components of the total personality—social, emotional, and intellectual—are somewhat vague. Although these are manifested in various ways, we do not actually see them as we do the physical aspect. Consequently, it becomes very important that during childhood a serious attempt be made to gain control over the physical aspect, or basic body control. The ability to do this, of course, will vary from one person to another. It will depend to a large extent upon physical fitness.

The broad area of physical fitness can be broken down into certain components, and it is important that individuals achieve to the best of their natural ability as far as these components are concerned. There is not complete agreement on identification of physical fitness components. However, the following can be considered as basic:

1. *Muscular strength:* This refers to the contraction power of muscles. The strength of muscles is usually measured with dynamometers or tensiometers, which record the amount of force particular muscle groups can apply in a single maximum effort. Humans' existence and effectiveness depend upon muscles. All movements of the body or any of its parts are impossible without action by muscles attached to the skeleton. Muscles perform vital functions of the body as well. The heart is a muscle; death occurs when it ceases to contract. Breathing, digestion, and elimination are dependent upon muscular contractions. These vital muscular functions are influenced by exercising the skeletal muscles; the heart beats faster, the blood circulates through the body at a greater rate, breathing becomes deep and rapid, and perspiration breaks out on the skin's surface.

2. *Muscular endurance:* Muscular endurance is the ability of muscles to perform work. Two variations of muscular endurance are recognized: *isometric,* whereby a maximum muscular contraction is held, and *isotonic,* whereby the muscles continue to raise and lower a submaximal load as in weight training or performing push-ups. In the isometric form, the muscles maintain a fixed length; in the isotonic form, they alternatively shorten and lengthen. Muscular endurance must assume some muscular strength. However, there are distinctions between the two; muscle groups of the same strength may possess different degrees of endurance.

3. *Circulatory-respiratory endurance:* Circulatory-respiratory endurance is characterized by moderate contractions of large muscle groups for relatively long periods of time, during which maximal adjustments of the circulatory-respiratory system to the activity are necessary, as in distance running and swimming. Obviously, strong and enduring muscles are needed. However,

by themselves they are not enough; they do not guarantee well-developed circulatory-respiratory functions.

As far as the physical aspect of personality is concerned, a major objective of human beings should be directed to maintaining a suitable level of physical fitness. This is the topic of the following discussion.

MAINTAINING A SUITABLE LEVEL OF PHYSICAL FITNESS

Physical fitness presupposes an adequate intake of good food and an adequate amount of rest and sleep, but beyond these things, activity involving all of the big muscles of the body is essential. Just how high a level of physical fitness should be maintained from one stage of life to another is difficult to ascertain because we must raise the following question: Fitness for what? Obviously, the young varsity athlete needs to think of a level of fitness far above that which will concern the average middle-aged individual.

Physical fitness has been described in different ways by different people. However, when all of these descriptions are put together it is likely that they will be characterized more by their similarities than their differences. For purposes here, physical fitness will be considered the human organism's level of ability to perform certain physical tasks or, stated another way, the fitness to perform various specified tasks requiring muscular effort.

An important question to raise at this point is: Why is a reasonably high level of physical fitness desirable in modern times when so many effort-saving devices are available that, for many people, strenuous activity is really not necessary anymore? One possible answer to this is that all of us stand at the end of a long line of ancestors, all of whom lived at least long enough to survive in the face of savage beasts and savage men, and all of whom were able to work hard. Only the strong and fit survived. Not very far back in your own family tree you will find people who had to be rugged and extremely active in order to live. Vigorous action and physical ruggedness are our biological heritage. Possibly because of the kind of background that humans have, our bodies simply function better when we are active.

Most child development specialists agree that vigorous play in childhood is essential for the satisfactory growth of the various organs and systems of the body. It has been said that "play is the business of childhood." To conduct this "business" successfully and happily, the child should be physically fit. Good nutrition, rest, and properly conducted physical activities in school can do much to develop and maintain the physical fitness of children and youth. Continuing this practice throughout life should be an essential goal for all people.

The word *exercise* may tend to have strong moralistic overtones. Like so many things that are said to be good for you, it also tends to give rise to certain feelings of boredom and resentment. Thus, some people draw more than facetious pleasure in repeating the old sayings "When I feel like exercising, I lie down quickly until the feeling goes away" and "I get my exercise serving as pallbearer for my friends who exercised."

As a former physical education teacher, I can summarize my feelings about exercising and maintaining some level of physical fitness by saying that doing so makes possible meaningful experiences in life that are not otherwise available. These experiences include all kinds of physical activity and exercise, including indoor and outdoor sports, and they also include the rich and satisfying interpersonal relationships usually associated with these activities. In addition, maintaining some level of physical fitness has still another value that is usually not fully appreciated. This value has to do with the idea that the entire personality of every individual rests upon, and is dependent on, its physical base. The entire personality—which is to say, all of the social, emotional, and intellectual components—is threatened when the physical component, the base of operation, is weak or unreliable. Fitness enthusiasts have claimed that academic performance, emotional control, and social adjustments are improved when an adequate level of physical fitness is improved, and many case histories and clinical data would tend to support this contention. It could be argued that a reasonably solid physical base is more likely than an unstable one to serve you as a successful launching pad for other personality resources. In other words, you will likely do better in everything you undertake if you feel good, your vitality is high, and you are capable of prolonged effort.

BODY TYPES AND SEGMENTS, AND PHYSICAL FITNESS

Body Types

Fundamental to understanding yourself is understanding the structure and proportions of your own body. Body builds have been classified in several ways, but they reduce to three major types: (1) the heavy, broad-hipped, relatively narrow-shouldered type (endomorph); (2) the broad-shouldered, narrow-hipped muscular type (mesomorph); and (3) the lean, straight-up-and-down type (ectomorph). Of course, the "average" woman is not the same as the "average" man, but the same general classifications apply to both sexes.

Interestingly, these body types are associated with different emotions and behaviors. For example, the endomorph is said to be jovial, enjoys eating and sensual pleasures and tends to be extroverted (viscerotonic). The mesomorph is competitive, aggressive, and enjoys athletics and tends to be ambiverted (musculoskeletonic). The ectomorph is serious, intellectual, enjoys reading, and tends to be introverted (cerebrotonic). Anyone can deviate from the standard.

Occasionally individuals approach being "pure types" in the sense of being true to one type. However, most people are mixtures of the first and second type (endomorph-mesomorph) or of the second and third type (mesomorph-ectomorph). For example, people can have an upper body of one type and a lower body of another. By way of illustration, take the case of an individual who was somewhat self-conscious and uncomfortable about having what seemed to him to be mesomorphic arms and trunk on relatively ectomorphic legs. However, it occurred to him one day that the present arrangement somehow served him quite well, or at least did not prevent his doing most of the things he wanted to do, so he stopped worrying about it.

Heredity, chance blending of genes, and undoubtedly other factors not completely known to us determine our basic body types. This being the case, individuals must decide to accept their body types because they can do little to change the basic structure.

Learn to make the most of what you have. No matter what type body you may have, you can elevate it to, or maintain it at, a satisfactory level of physical fitness. Even though you should happen to be very endomorphic or ectomorphic, you can be strong, have good endurance, and learn to be skillful in the activities that you like. Most heavily built people can control their weight by minimizing the starches and fats in their diets and exercising regularly. Most lean people can elevate their weight, putting it on "in the right places," by following the basic recommendations for increasing their protein and carbohydrate food intake reasonably high. Even if the weight does not increase, the main point is that one feels well enough and enjoys the things he or she likes to do.

No matter what your own particular body type, you can participate successfully in most activity programs in which the emphasis is on having an active, pleasurable experience. However, if you wish to excel in a sport, you should pick one that suits your body type. Of course, the athletic type (mesomorph) stands to have a chance in most sports, but his or her weight and leanings toward endomorphy or ectomorphy are important factors that determine where he or she is likely to perform the best. However, the well-developed lean individual (ectomorph) tends to excel in noncontact sports such as middle- and long-distance running and tennis. The well-muscled heavy person (endomorph) has a chance in such sports as football (lineman, for example), and often excels in distance swimming where buoyancy and insulation against cold may be a major advantage. Some individuals of high endomorphic components have been outstanding weight lifters and heavyweight wrestlers.

One's body type should not exclude him or her from all recreational sports. At the highly competitive level, the athletic types have the greatest range of possibilities open to them; however, the interested endomorph or ectomorph has opportunities too.

Body Segments

The sizes of the various body segments have an important bearing upon physical performance. For example, even though two men have equal leg length, other things being equal, the one with the longer legs often will win a race because the longer stride provides a mechanical advantage. In effect, he is able to go into high gear while the shorter man must roar along in low. However, probably of greater interest to the average person is the role of the size of the various segments of the body in determining one's bigness or smallness. If you have several people of about the same size sit on the edge of a desk and compare the length of their necks, trunks, upper legs, and lower legs, you will probably find that these measurements vary widely from person to person. It is likely that one person may have the height in one segment of the body while another may have it in a different segment. Thus, some tall men and women are really not big anywhere except in their long bones. Some short people are just as big as their friends, except that their necks are short.

By tradition, North Americans seem to equate bigness with "bestness." Because we might have the biggest buildings and biggest cities, drive the biggest cars, and so on, we feel somehow superior. Similarly, this is true of bigness in people, especially men—although tall, long-legged women receive attention too. The point is that this "bigness is best" idea is a completely arbitrary standard that does not necessarily have any bearing upon either the quality of the car or the humanness of the person. Moreover, when we consider that one's bigness or smallness may be entirely a matter of long lower leg bones, the whole business begins to seem relatively unimportant. Incidentally, these arbitrary standards of what is best for people sometimes gets pretty complicated. Some individuals not only tend to prize bigness but not being very "different" as well. Thus, one is about as likely to be considered an "oddball" if he or she is very bright or quite dull. People like to fit comfortably within the "norms" our various statisticians calculate for us. Related to this, before basketball made it permissible for men (and women) to be very tall, tall young men and women sometimes had poor posture because they were forever slouching down so as to appear "normal."

It is, of course, possible, within limits, to cultivate one's body, to make it serviceable and reasonably attractive by keeping it fit and learning to use it with skill. People should be inclined to consider doing so on a par with "cultivating the mind." To repeat the opening comments in this general discussion—understanding and accepting our bodies as they are, including those aspects that we can do something about, are fundamental factors in accepting ourselves as human beings whose personalities are our own and not really the business of arbitrary standardization.

TYPES OF EXERCISE

Generally speaking, there are three types of exercises: (1) proprioceptive-facilitative, (2) isotonic, and (3) isometric. (In reading this section of the chapter the reader is asked to reflect back to the discussion of the components of physical fitness—muscular strength, muscular endurance, and circulatory-respiratory endurance.)

Proprioceptive-Facilitative Exercises

These exercises consist of various refined patterns of movement. Important in the performance of these exercises are those factors involved in movement: (1) time, (2) force, (3) space, and (4) flow.

Time is concerned with how long it takes to complete a movement. For example, a movement can be slow and deliberate, such as a child attempting to create a body movement to depict a falling snowflake. On the other hand, a movement might be made with sudden quickness, such as starting to run for a goal on a signal.

Force needs to be applied to set the body or one of its segments in motion and to change its speed and/or direction. Thus, force is concerned with how much strength is required for movement. Swinging the arms requires less strength than attempting to propel the body over the surface area with a standing long jump.

In general, two factors are concerned with *space*. These are the amount of space required to perform a particular movement and the utilization of available space.

All movements involve some degree of rhythm in their performance. Thus, *flow* is the sequence of movement involving rhythmic motion.

These four factors are included in all body movements in various degrees. The degree to which each is used effectively in combination will determine the extent to which the movement is performed with skill. This is a basic essential in the performance of proprioceptive-facilitative exercises. In addition, various combinations of the following are involved in the performance of this type of exercise.

1. *Muscular power:* Ability to release maximum muscular force in the shortest time. Example: Standing long jump.
2. *Agility:* Speed in changing body position or in changing direction. Example: dodging run.

3. *Speed:* Rapidity with which successive movements of the same kind can be performed. Example: fifty-yard dash.
4. *Flexibility:* Range of movement in a joint or sequence of joints. Example: Touch the floor with fingers without bending the knees.
5. *Balance:* Ability to maintain position and equilibrium both in movement (dynamic balance) and while stationary (static balance). Examples: Walking on a line or balance beam (dynamic); standing on one foot (static).
6. *Coordination:* Working together of the muscles and organs of the body in the performance of a specific task. Example: Throwing or catching an object.

Isotonic Exercises

These are the familiar types of exercises. An isotonic exercise involves the amount of resistance one can overcome during one application of force through the full range of motion in a given joint or joints. An example of this would be picking up a weight and flexing the elbows while lifting the weight to shoulder height.

Isotonics can improve strength to some extent. They also are very useful for increasing and maintaining full range of motion. Such range of motion should be maintained throughout life if possible, although it can decrease with age with such musculoskeletal disorders as arthritis. This disease can cause shortening of fibrous tissue structures and this is likely to limit the normal range of motion.

Another important feature of isotonic exercise is that it can increase circulatory-respiratory endurance in such activities as running (jogging) and swimming.

Isometric Exercises

Although isometrics do not provide much in the way of improvement of normal range of motion and endurance, they are most useful in increasing strength and volume of muscles. In isometrics the muscle is contracted, but the length of the muscle is generally the same during contraction as during relaxation. The contraction is accomplished by keeping two joints rigid while contracting the muscle(s) between the joints. A maximal amount of force is applied against a fixed resistance during one all-out effort. An example of this is pushing or pulling against an immovable object. If you place your hands against a wall and push with as much force as you can, you have effected the contraction of certain muscles while their length has remained essentially the same.

DEVELOPING AN ACTIVITY PROGRAM

In recommending physical activity—vigorous, pleasurable physical activity—to adults and children, I am doing so not only in the sense that it will be likely to reduce, eliminate, or, avoid chronic fatigue and lessen the impact of acute fatigue. I recommend it, too, on the basis that the ability to move the body skillfully in a variety of ways and for appropriate periods of time is a dimension of human experience that is fundamental, pleasurable, and meaningful. It is part of being human and alive.

The traditional recommendation has been to consult a physician before undertaking a physical activity program. It is likely that a physician will recommend the program without restriction, or if a problem is found, he or she will take steps to correct it—and may make suggestions for modifying the program to make it more suitable to you as an individual.

A program should be an individual matter and one that fits one's own needs and wishes. In other words, if a person is not happy with the program, it will be unlikely that it will meet with success as far as personal goals are concerned. Each individual will have to determine which particular approach is best for him or her: specified exercises, recreational sports, or a combination of both. Three important factors need consideration when formulating an exercise program: (1) *frequency,* (2) *persistence,* and (3) *positive reinforcement.*

Once the exercise program is decided, whether prescribed exercises or recreational sports, the next thing is to determine how many times per week to engage in these activities. It is best to avoid the extremes of the "once in a while" or "always without fail" spurts and try to maintain a regular schedule of three or four times per week. It is also a good idea to work out on alternate days—Monday, Wednesday, and Friday, or Tuesday, Thursday, and Saturday. The hour of the day does not necessarily matter. However, if the fitness program is going to be high on a priority list, it should not be difficult to get into the habit of putting regular workouts into a weekly schedule.

Persistence and adherence are as important to any exercise program as the activities or exercises themselves. Much better and longer-lasting results will be obtained from a program of three or four steady and regular workouts each week than a program where one exercises intensely every day for a week and then does nothing at all for the following two or three weeks. Once the desired level of fitness has been reached, a maintenance program might be less strenuous and/or slightly less frequent.

Psychological research has determined that a response that is reinforced is more apt to be repeated than one that is not. When this kind of research was first conducted, it was thought that the reward of desired behavior and the punishment of undesired behavior created equal and opposite effects. It was quickly discovered that this was not the case. Punishment seems to have a less permanent effect than reward, and punishment may even bring about the opposite results from those intended. Therefore, we are seeking positive reinforcement. Although plenty of positive reinforcement seems to be built into a fitness program (looking and feeling better), praise and encouragement should be forthcoming from others. This also works both ways. If some members of a family are attempting to change their fitness condition, by all means encouragement and praise should be offered. Obviously, it should go without saying that criticizing or belittling are the easiest way to put a damper on, or even wipe out completely, a person's confidence and enthusiasm for a fitness program.

IMPORTANCE OF PHYSICAL EXERCISE IN REDUCING STRESS

Exercise can provide a variety of stress reduction benefits for many individuals. Many people under stress experience a fight-or-flight response characterized by increased muscle tension, blood pressure, and heart rate due to the release of stress-related hormones and increased sympathetic-nervous-system activities. These are designed to increase alertness and improve strength for fight, or greater speed for flight. However, if this state persists or is not followed by a period of relaxation, a variety of physical and emotional problems can ensue. Exercise may relieve stress by providing an outlet for increased energy stores that have not been utilized. In some instances, exercise may provide emotional benefits, as stressful thoughts are replaced by focusing on the activity being pursued. Endorphin secretion may increase, promoting a sense of well-being or euphoria, and greater resistance to pain. We often hear of the "runner's high" and people feeling good about themselves after exercising. When we stop exercising, heart rate and blood pressure fall, breathing becomes slower and more regular, and muscle tension is dissipated. In addition, during the postexercise period, we are apt to fall into a relaxed and contemplative state that provides other emotional benefits.

For years the value of exercise as a means of reducing stress has been documented by various sources. Walter McQuade and Ann Aikman[1] once suggested that one of the many stresses people suffer from is stress resulting from their own pent-up aggressiveness. When people express these drives through physical action, they benefit because exercise not only dispels this form of stress, but it also enables the body to fight stress in general.

Similarly, Beata Jencks[2] once reported that physical and emotional trauma upset the balance of body and mind, and that much energy is wasted in muscular tension, bringing on unnecessary tiredness and exhaustion. This could mean that if stress reactions become habit patterns, then the muscles and tendons shorten and thicken and excessive connective tissue is deposited, causing a general consolidation of tissues. As mentioned previously, excess energy released by action of the sympathetic nervous system, if not immediately dissipated by muscular action, produces muscular tension. This tension can be relieved through muscular action in the form of exercise.

From a different perspective, C. Eugene Walker[3] suggested that exercise is very effective in reducing anxiety. He theorized that it may satisfy the human evolutionary need to engage in large-muscle, physically aggressive activity that was very adaptive for primitive man, but with highly civilized, sedentary, and confined lifestyle, has fewer acceptable outlets.

As far as objective scientific inquiry is concerned, a number of controlled studies provide evidence that physical activity contributes to one's capacity to reduce stress. One representative example is the early work of Richard Driscoll.[4] He studied the effect of forty minutes of stress treatment and a combination of physical exertion and positive imagery upon anxiety. High-anxiety students were tested in six conditions, including one group that received standard systematic desensitization (a form of behavior modification), one that received the exercise and imagery treatment, and a control group that received no treatment. After witnessing a sequence of stressful scenes, the group that was most successful in effectively reducing anxiety was the one that used the physical exertion of running, plus positive imagery of themselves being calm and tranquil. Driscoll found that the combination of positive imagery and physical exertion produced the greatest reduction of anxiety. This study is supportive of other evidence that suggests stress reduction means simply giving one an acceptable way of recovering from a stressful incident.

PHYSICAL ACTIVITY FOR CHILDREN

One of the most important characteristics of life is movement. Whatever else they may involve, practically all of our achievements are based on our ability to move. Obviously, the very young child is not a highly evolved being in the sense of abstract thinking; he or she only gradually acquires the ability to deal with symbols and intellectualize experiences in the course of development. On the other hand, children are creatures of movement. Any effort to help the child grow, develop, learn, and be reasonably free from stress and tension must take the importance of movement into account.

Practically all children—unless there is an incapacitating impairment—will engage in physical activity if given the opportunity to do so. They run, jump, climb, and play games requiring these movement skills. Some adults consider this so-called "free play" meaningless. On the contrary, it is very meaningful to children as they explore various ways to move their bodies through space. In addition to this unorganized form of activity, there are various types of organized physical activity programs for children. In general, these can be classified into the two broad categories of school programs and out-of-school programs.

School Programs

Most above-average elementary schools try to provide well-balanced physical education programs for children. Just as young children need to learn the skills of reading, writing, and mathematics, they should also learn the basic physical skills. These include: (1) locomotor skills of walking, running, leaping, jumping, hopping, galloping, skipping, and sliding; (2) the auxiliary skills of starting, stopping, dodging, pivoting, landing, and falling; and (3) the skills of propulsion and retrieval involving throwing, striking, kicking, and catching.

For the young child, being able to move as effectively and efficiently as possible is directly related to the proficiency with which he or she will be able to perform the various fundamental physical skills. In turn, the success that children have in physical activities requiring certain motor skills will be dependent upon their proficiency of performance of these skills. Thus, effective and efficient movement is a prerequisite to the performance of basic motor skills needed for success in school physical education activities. These activities include active games, rhythmic activities, and gymnastic activities. (Parents are advised to explore the extent to which a given school provides for such physical activities for children.)

Exercises for Stressful Classroom Situations

Although exercises for stressful classroom situations are not a part of the organized school program, they are useful in helping children deal with stress in the regular classroom situation. As mentioned previously, many stressful conditions can prevail in the school environment. The present discussion is concerned with the child's active behavior in a stressful situation. More specifically, what exercises can teachers provide children to help them deal with a stressful situation in the classroom?

Various authentic pronouncements have been made that support the idea that instant activity can be beneficial. Being engaged in activity, rather than remaining passive, is preferred by most individuals in stressful situations and can be highly effective in reducing stress. Also, a person may alter his or her psychological and physiological stress reactions in a given situation simply by taking action, and this,

in turn, will affect his or her appraisal of the situation, thereby ultimately altering the stress reaction.

What, then, are some of the physical exercises that teachers can
have children engage in as a reaction to a stressful situation? Obviously, it would not seem to be appropriate to engage in isotonics by
dropping to the floor and start doing push-ups or to break into a jog
around the room. Isometrics are recommended for this purpose and
the following are some possibilities. Certainly, creative teachers will
be able to think of others.

1. *Hand and head press:* Interweave fingers and place hands at
   the back of the head with elbows pointing out. Push the head
   backward on the hands while simultaneously pulling the head
   forward with the hands. This can be done while standing or
   sitting at a desk.
2. *Wall press:* Stand with the back against the wall. Allow the
   arms to hang down at the sides. Turn hands toward the wall
   and press the wall with the palms, keeping the arms straight.
3. *Hand pull:* Bend the right elbow and bring the right hand in
   with the palm up close to the front of the body. Put the left
   hand in the right hand. Try to curl the right arm upward while
   simultaneously resisting with the left hand. Repeat, using the
   opposite pressure. This can be done while standing or sitting
   at a desk.
4. *Hand push:* The hands are clasped with the palms together
   close to the chest with the elbows pointing out. Press the
   hands together firmly.
5. *Leg press:* While sitting at a desk or table, cross the left ankle
   over the right ankle. The feet are on the floor and the legs are
   at approximately a right angle. Try to straighten the right leg
   while resisting with the left leg. Repeat with the right angle
   over the left ankle.
6. *The gripper:* Place one hand in the other and grip hard. Another variation is to grip an object. While standing, this could
   be the back of a chair or, while sitting, it could be the arms of a
   chair or the seat.
7. *Chair push:* While sitting at a desk or table with the hands on
   the armrests of the chair, push down with the hands. The entire

buttocks can be raised from the chair seat. One or both feet can be lifted off the floor, or both can remain in contact with the floor.

8. *Hip lifter:* While sitting at a desk or table, lift one buttock after the other from the chair seat. Try to keep the head from moving. The hands can be placed at the sides of the chair seat for balance.

9. *Heel and toe:* From a standing position, rise on the toes. Come back down on the heels while raising both the toes and the balls of the feet.

10. *Fist clencher:* Clench fists and then open the hands, extending the fingers as far as possible.

This short list is comprised of representative examples of isometric exercises, and they are actually referred to by some as *stress exercises.* Although it has been recommended that these types of exercises can be performed easily in the school environment, it is obvious that they can be performed elsewhere as well. Wherever they are performed, the principle of tensing-releasing should be applied. That is, tense briefly and then release. (This will be discussed in detail in Chapter 10.)

The isometric exercises recommended here have met with success when teachers had children perform them in stressful school situations.

Out-of-School Programs

Out-of-school programs are provided by various organizations such as boys' and girls' clubs and neighborhood recreation centers. These programs vary in quality depending upon the extent of suitable facilities and qualified personnel available to supervise and conduct them. Parents should investigate these programs thoroughly to make sure they are being conducted in the best interests of children. Some highly competitive sports programs for children place more emphasis on adult pride than on the welfare of children. This should not be interpreted as an indictment against all out-of-school programs because many of them are doing a satisfactory job.

Some families do not rely on any kind of organized out-of-school program, preferring instead to plan their own activities. This is commendable because it can result in fine family relationships as well as provide for wholesome physical activity for the entire family.

Chapter 9

Body Restoration and Stress

In the present context, the term *body restoration* means "the relief of and/or the recovery from fatigue through the process of rest and sleep." To be effective and enjoy life to the utmost, adults and children need periodic recuperation; it is an essential ingredient in our daily living pattern. Rest and sleep provide us with the means of revitalizing ourselves so we can meet the challenges of our responsibilities.

FATIGUE

Any consideration given to body restoration should perhaps begin with a discussion of fatigue. In order to keep fatigue at a minimum and in its proper proportion in the cycle of everyday activities, nature has provided us with ways to help combat and reduce fatigue. First, however, we should consider what fatigue is so that it may be easier for us to cope with it. There are two types of fatigue—acute and chronic.

Acute Fatigue

Acute fatigue is a natural outcome of sustained or severe exertion. It is due to such physical factors as the accumulation of by-products of muscular exertion in the blood and excessive oxygen debt—the inability of the body to take in as much oxygen as is being consumed by muscular work. Psychological considerations may also be important in acute fatigue. For example, an individual who becomes bored with what he or she is doing and who becomes preoccupied with the discomfort involved will become fatigued much sooner than if he or she is highly motivated to do the same thing, is not bored, and does not think about the discomfort.

Activity that brings about distressing fatigue in one individual may amount to mild, even pleasant exertion for another. The difference in fatigue levels is due essentially to differences in physical fitness levels or in training. For example, a good walker or dancer may soon become fatigued when running or swimming hard. The key, then, to controlling and preventing premature and undue fatigue is sufficient training in the activities to be engaged in. Knowing one's limits at any given time is also important for avoiding excessively fatiguing exertion and for determining what preparatory training is necessary. Adults must be on the lookout for any fatigue symptoms in children.

Chronic Fatigue

Chronic fatigue is fatigue that lasts over extended periods—in contrast to acute fatigue which tends to be followed by a recovery phase and restoration to "normal" within a relatively brief period of time. Chronic fatigue may be due to a variety of medical conditions ranging from disease to malnutrition. (Such conditions are the concern of the physician, who should evaluate all cases of chronic fatigue to ensure that disease is not responsible for the condition.) Chronic fatigue may also be due to psychological factors such as extreme boredom and/or worry about having to do, over an extended period, what one does not wish to do.

REST

In general, most people think of rest as just "taking it easy." A chief purpose of rest is to reduce tension so that the body may be better able to recover from fatigue. No overt activity is involved in rest, but neither is there loss of consciousness or loss of awareness of the external environment as in sleep. Since the need for rest is usually in direct proportion to the exertion required in the activity in which one is engaged, it follows naturally that the more strenuous the activity, the more frequent the rest periods should be. A busy day at school may not be as noticeably tiring as a game of tennis; nevertheless, the wise person will let the body dictate when a rest period is required. Five or ten minutes of sitting in a chair with the eyes closed may make the difference in the course of an active day. The effectiveness of rest periods for children depends largely on the individual child and his or her ability to relax.

SLEEP

Sleep is a phenomenon that has never been clearly and completely defined or understood, but it has aptly been named the "great restorer," and an old Welsh proverb states that "disease and sleep are far apart." Authorities on the subject agree that sleep is essential to the vital functioning of the body and that natural sleep is the most satisfying method of recuperating from fatigue. During sleep, the body is given an opportunity to revitalize itself. All vital functions are slowed down so that the building of new cells and the repair of tissues can take place without undue interruption. This does not mean that the body builds and regenerates tissues only during sleep, but, rather, that sleep is the time that nature has set aside to accomplish the task more easily. During sleep, the body's metabolic rate is lowered and energy is restored.

Although various theories have been advanced regarding the nature of sleep, scientists still know very little about what sleep really is or what it accomplishes on a molecular level. It has been reported that sleep helps rid the brain of a chemical called *adenosine* that builds up during wakeful hours, but no one is sure why adenosine must be eliminated, or what other brain chemicals may contribute to the subjective feelings of sleepiness or mental exhaustion.[1]

Experts have suggested that, on average, we do not get enough sleep. For example, Richard Allen, co-director of the Johns Hopkins University Sleep Disorders Center, has been quoted as saying, "There's a fairly pervasive lack of adequate sleep in our society, which leads to problems with alertness and life satisfaction." He emphasized further that "the quantity of wakefulness may be increased but the quality is decreased."[2]

One estimate states that 100 million Americans do not get a good night's sleep on a regular basis. In addition, throughout the world, an even larger number of people live in a chronic state of sleep deprivation.[3] Yet, ironically, a recent report suggested that people who sleep six or seven hours per night actually live longer than people who sleep eight or more.[4] It is doubtful that prominent sleep researchers would agree with this claim since most of them recommend that we get *more* sleep, not less.

With need for sleep having been acknowledged, a question of paramount importance remains. How much sleep is necessary for the body to accomplish its recuperative task? There is no clear-cut answer to this query. Sleep is an individual matter, based on degree rather than kind. The usual recommendation for adults is eight hours of sleep in every twenty-four period, but this is a generalization. Many people can function effectively on less sleep, while others require more. (Required hours of sleep are, of course, higher for children at the different age levels.) No matter how many hours of sleep one gets during the course of a twenty-four-hour period, the best test of adequacy could be how one feels. If one is normally alert, feels healthy, and is in good humor, he or she is probably getting sufficient sleep. The rest that sleep brings to the body depends to a large extent on a person's freedom from excessive emotional tension and his or her ability to relax. Unrelaxed sleep has little restorative value, but learning to relax is a skill that is not acquired in one night.

Is loss of sleep dangerous? This is a question that is pondered quite frequently. Again, the answer is not simple. To the healthy person with normal sleep habits, occasionally losing hours of sleep is not serious. On the other hand, repeated loss of sleep over a period of time can be dangerous. It is the loss of sleep night after night, rather than at one time, that apparently does the damage and results in chronic fatigue. The general effects of frequent loss of sleep are poor general health, nervousness, irritability, inability to concentrate, lower perseverance of effort, and serious fatigue. Alert teachers can quickly recognize those children who are getting an insufficient amount of sleep at home.

Studies have shown that a person can go for much longer periods without food than without sleep. In some instances, successive nights of losing sleep for long periods have proven fatal. Under normal conditions, however, a night of lost sleep followed by a period of prolonged sleep will restore the individual to his or her normal self.

Many conditions may rob the body of restful slumber, including mental anguish and worry. So-called insomniacs may only think they are insomniacs, and an insomniac worries incessantly about his or her sleepless condition. A chronic insomniac is one who takes longer to fall asleep, has more trouble staying asleep, and wakes up earlier than a normal sleeper, feeling tired as a result. At any rate, cases of insomnia and chronic fatigue should be brought to the attention of a physician so that necessary steps can be taken to restore normal sleep patterns. Drugs to induce sleep should be used only if prescribed by a physician.

Memory, Brain Function, and Sleep

With regard to memory and brain function, a survey[5] of more than 1,000 adults revealed that few understood the important role that sleep plays in maintaining normal daily brain functions, especially memory. Almost half were under the impression that sleep allows the brain to rest. Actually, some parts of the brain may be more active when one is sleeping. While asleep, the brain classifies and prioritizes all this accumulated information, filing it for ready retrieval. This process begins with a retrospective review of the day's events, and can result in traveling back in time, so that by morning, one may be immersed in childhood memories.

In addition to memory, sleep is also critical in maintaining concentrating, learning, and performance skills. The majority of those surveyed admitted that their mental capacities suffered when they did not sleep well. In those that said that lack of sleep affected them more mentally than physically, 40 percent cited increased stress as their greatest problem, and this was particularly true for women.

When one does not get enough sleep, the ability to move information from short-term memory to long-term storage becomes impaired. For example, students who sleep several hours before cramming for an examination retain much more information than those who do not. If one needs to resolve a problem, or make an important decision, "sleeping on it" is probably a good idea.

Sleep and the Heart

Many heart attack patients experience insomnia in the period immediately prior to the event. The quality and type of sleep may also be important, since certain sleep states have been found to be associated with severe disturbance in cardiac rhythm, as well as heart attacks. These are particularly apt to occur during the *rapid eye move-*

ment (REM) phase of sleep, which is associated with dreaming. REM sleep is most frequent in the period immediately before spontaneously awakening in the morning, and is accompanied by a rise in sympathetic nervous system activity and secretion of stress-related hormones, resulting in increased blood pressure, heart rate, platelet clumping, and clot formation. One report[6] suggests that this could explain why many heart attacks occur between 6 a.m. and 11 a.m.

Sleep and Stress

As mentioned previously, millions of people suffer from some sort of sleep disorder. Millions also have periodic insomnia that is frequently stress related. Sleep deprivation for many is due to excessively long work hours, rotating shifts, last-minute preparation for meetings, unexpected events such as the loss of a close family member, and, of course, for students, preparing for examinations.

Working parents may not get enough sleep because of the stress of hectic schedules or the need to awaken frequently for child care duties.

Although most people require seven or eight hours of sleep each night, my own studies reveal that probably one-half of us get as much sleep as we need. This can lead to problems with alertness and life satisfaction.

Stress is the leading cause of temporary insomnia, and chronic insomnia is common in almost every patient with persistent depression, which is often stress related. Just as stress is a major cause of insomnia, lack of sleep is an important source of stress for many individuals. In addition to irritability and fatigue, chronic sleep deprivation can contribute to many disorders. These disorders can generate additional stress that in turn, interferes with sleep.

Getting a Good Night's Sleep

Various recommendations could be made for getting a good night's sleep. Many conditions rob the body of restful slumber. Most certainly, mental anguish and worry play a very large part in decreasing or interrupting sleep. Some factors that influence the quality of sleep are hunger, a cold environment, boredom, and excessive fatigue. In many instances these factors can be controlled. We need to think of this in two ways: things *not* to do as well as things *to* do. Although hunger could be an influence on quality of sleep, at the same time overeating near bedtime can interfere with sleep. Being "too full" can possibly cause digestive problems and keep one awake. Of course, a little warm milk often can serve as a suitable tranquilizer.

It is generally recommended that one not have any food containing caffeine several hours before going to bed. The same can be said for alcoholic beverages. Although they may make one feel drowsy, the quality of sleep is likely to be disturbed.

An important factor in getting a good night's rest is the sleep environment; conditions should be comfortable for satisfying sleep. We often hear about "good sleeping weather," which really means having the room at a suitable temperature. A general recommendation is that the room temperature be between 65 and 68 degrees Fahrenheit. However, this is an individual matter and one can adjust to the temperature found most suitable.

Those seeking consistently restful sleep should follow a specific routine. The process should be the same each night, and should begin at the same hour, leading to repose at about the same time. That is, if your bedtime is normally ten o'clock, your preparation should perhaps begin as early as nine-thirty and possibly by nine o'clock. You might wish to stop what you are doing at least one-half hour before the fixed time to retire.

The importance of sleep as a gold mine of research is evidenced by existence of an organization called the Associated Professional Sleep Societies. In addition, there are approximately 150 accredited sleep centers throughout the United States.

CHILDREN'S SLEEP HABITS

During the first year of a child's life, it is common to have two nap periods, one in the morning and one in the afternoon. The one-year-old child gradually gives up the morning nap, and this tends to increase the afternoon nap time as well as the night sleep. With age, the afternoon nap time will decrease and, as a consequence, the child will sleep longer at night. Although there is some difference of opinion on when a child should give up both the morning and afternoon naps, it is generally recommended that preschoolers have at least one nap per day, preferably in the afternoon.

Perhaps at this point it should be mentioned that napping is an activity that is not exclusively reserved for children. In fact, when studying about job stress my survey of several employers found that some of them actually provided "nap rooms" for employees. They believed that a short nap at the appropriate time resulted in improved work performance. William A. Anthony, professor of psychology at Boston University, wrote in detail on the concept of napping.[7]

As in the case of adults, school-aged children differ in the amount of sleep they require. The general recommendation calls for ten hours of sleep out of every twenty-four hours. Bedtime should be a happy time. Parents should not make such an issue of the child going to bed that conflict results. Perhaps a good rule for a younger child is that he or she be "taken" to bed rather than "sent" to bed. The ritual of reading or telling a child a pleasant story at bedtime is important and can help lessen the impact of sudden separation. Some sleep disorders of children, such as nightmares and bed-wetting, can be traced directly to stressful or traumatic separation at bedtime.

Studies show that being rested translates into better grades.[8] In this regard the National Heart, Lung, and Blood Institute recommends that parents should:

- Set times to sleep and wake up on school days.
- Avoid big meals close to bedtime, and limit sugar and caffeine for six hours before bed.
- Establish a relaxing bedtime routine with time to wind down. (Avoid video games or TV before bedtime, which make children hyperactive, interfering with sleep.)
- Make the room dark and quiet. (A night-light can help if a child is afraid of the dark.)

Understanding the complex nature of sleep may be the province of scientists and other qualified experts, but an understanding of the value of sleep is the responsibility of everyone.

Chapter 10

Reducing Stress Through Relaxation

Relax! How many times have you heard this expression? Although it has frequent usage as a means of telling a person to "take it easy," often those using the expression are not aware of its real meaning. Most of us need some form of relaxation to relieve the tensions encountered in daily living. The purpose of this chapter is to explore various facets of relaxation, along with conditions that produce a relaxed state both for children and adults.

Many procedures can help improve a person's ability to relax, and thus reduce stress. However, what may be satisfactory for one person may not necessarily be so for another.

THE MEANING OF RELAXATION AND RELATED TERMS

In general, there are two types of relaxation—passive relaxation and deep muscle relaxation. Passive relaxation involves such activities as reading and listening to music. In deep muscle relaxation the muscle fibers have one function—they contract. This is the response they make to the electrochemical stimulation of impulses carried via the motor nerves. Relaxation is the removal of this stimulation.

The term *relaxation response* was introduced several years ago by Herbert Benson[1] of Harvard University and it involves a number of bodily changes that occur in the organism when one experiences deep muscle relaxation. A response against "overstress" brings on these bodily changes and returns the body to a healthier balance. Thus, the purpose of any kind of relaxation should be to induce a relaxation response.

Chapters 11 and 12 will discuss the stress reduction techniques of *meditation* and *biofeedback,* both of which can indeed be considered relaxation techniques. Therefore, attention should be given to the theory underlying these techniques, all of which are concerned with mind-body interactions and designed to induce the relaxation response. In *progressive relaxation,* it is theorized that if the muscles of the body are relaxed, the mind in turn will be quieted. Meditation assumes that if the mind is quieted, then other systems of the body will tend to become more readily stabilized. In the practice of biofeedback, the theoretical basis tends to involve some sort of integration of progressive relaxation and meditation. It is believed that the brain has the potential for voluntary control over all the systems it monitors, and is affected by all of these systems. Thus, it is the intimacy of interaction between mind and body that has provided the mechanism through which one can learn voluntary control over biological activity.

From the physiologist's point of view, relaxation is sometimes considered zero activity, or as near zero as one can manage in the neuromuscular system. That is, it is a neuromuscular accomplishment that results in reduction, or possible complete absence, of muscle tone in a part of or in the entire body. A primary value of relaxation lies in the lowering of brain and spinal-cord activity, resulting from a reduction of nerve impulses arising in muscle spindles and other sense endings in muscles, tendons, and joint structures.

People often confuse the meanings of *relaxation, refreshment,* and *recreation.* Although all of these factors are important to the well-being of the human organism, they should not be used interchangeably. Refreshment is the result of an improved blood supply to the brain for "refreshment" from central fatigue and the muscles for the disposition of their waste products. This explains in part why mild muscular activity is good for overcoming the fatigue of sitting quietly (seventh-inning stretch) and for hastening recovery after strenuous exercise (an athlete continuing to run slowly for a short distance after a race).

Recreation may be described as the experience from which a person emerges with the feeling of being "re-created." No single activity is sure to bring this experience to all members of a group, nor is there assurance that an activity will provide recreation again for a given person because it did so the last time. These are more the marks of a psychological experience. An important essential requirement for a recreational activity is that it completely engross the individual; that is, it must engage his or her entire undivided attention. Recreation is really escape from the disintegrating effects of distraction to the healing effect of totally integrated activity. Experiences that produce this effect may range from a hard game of tennis to the reading of a comic strip.

Some individuals consider recreation and relaxation to be the same, which is not the case. Recreation can be considered a type of mental diversion that can be helpful in relieving tension. Although mental and muscular tensions are interrelated, it is in the muscle that the tension state is manifested.

For many years, recommendations have been made with regard to procedures individuals might apply in an effort to relax. Examples of some of these procedures are submitted in the ensuing discussions. In consideration of any relaxation technique, one very important factor needs to be considered: learning to relax is a skill. This skill is based on the kinesthetic awareness of *tonus* (the normal degree of contraction present in most muscles, which keep them always ready to function when needed). Unfortunately, very few of us practice this skill, probably because we are unware of how to go about it.

One of the first steps in learning to relax is to experience tension. That is, one should be sensitive to tensions that exist in the body. This can be accomplished by voluntarily contracting a given muscle group, first very strongly and then less and less. Emphasis should be placed on detecting the signal of tension as the first step in letting go, or relaxing.

You might wish to try the traditional experiment used to demonstrate this phenomenon. Raise one arm so that the palm of the hand is facing outward away from your face. Now, bend the wrist backward and try to point the fingers back toward your face and down toward the forearm. You should feel some strain at the wrist joint. You should also feel something else in the muscle; this is tension due to the muscle contracting the hand backward. Now, flop the hand forward with the fingers pointing downward and you will have accomplished a *tension-relaxation* cycle.

As in the case of any muscular skill, learning how to relax takes time and complete satisfaction should not be expected immediately. After a comfortable relaxation technique is found, increased practice should eventually achieve satisfactory results.

PROGRESSIVE RELAXATION

The technique of progressive relaxation was developed by Edmund Jacobson many years ago.[2] It is still the technique most often referred to in the literature and probably the one that has had the most widespread application. In this technique, the person concentrates on progressively relaxing one muscle group after another. The technique is based on the procedure of comparing the difference between tension and relaxation. As previously mentioned, one must sense the tension in order to get the feeling of relaxation.

Learning to relax is a skill that one can develop in applying the principles of progressive relaxation. One of the first steps is to be able to identify the various muscle groups and how to tense them so that tension and relaxation can be experienced. However, before making suggestions on how to tense and relax the various muscle groups certain preliminary measures need to be taken into account.

1. This procedure takes time and proficiency comes with practicing the skills.
2. Progressive relaxation is not to be done spontaneously. Be prepared to spend twenty to thirty minutes at a time in tensing-relaxing activities.
3. The particular time of day is important. This is an individual matter. Progressive relaxation can be practiced daily, preferably once during the day and again in the evening before retiring. For many people this would be difficult, unless one time period was set aside before going to school or work in the morning. This could be a good way to help a person start the day relaxed.
4. It is important to find a suitable place to practice the tensing-relaxation activities. Again, this is an individual matter with some preferring a bed or couch and others a comfortable chair.
5. Consideration should be given to the amount of time a given muscle is tensed, to be able to feel the difference between tension and relaxation. This means that tension should be maintained from four to not more than eight seconds.
6. Breathing is an important part in tensing and relaxing muscles. To begin, it is suggested that three or more deep breaths be taken and held for about five seconds. This will result in a better breathing rhythm. Controlled breathing makes it easier to relax

and is most effective when it is done deeply and slowly. It is ordinarily recommended that one should inhale deeply when the muscles are tensed and exhale slowly when relaxing the muscles.

How to Tense and Relax Various Muscles

Muscle groups may be identified in different ways. The classification given here consists of four different groups: (1) muscles of the head, face, tongue, and neck, (2) muscles of the trunk, (3) muscles of the upper extremities, and (4) muscles of the lower extremities.

Muscles of the Head, Face, Tongue, and Neck

There are two chief muscles of the head, the one covering the back of the head and the one covering the front of the skull. The face has approximately thirty muscles, including muscles of the orbit and eyelids, lips, tongue, and neck. Estimates indicate that it takes twenty-six facial muscles to frown and significantly fewer to smile.

Muscles of this group may be tensed and relaxed as follows (relaxation is accomplished by "letting go" after tensing):

1. Raise your right eyebrow by opening the eye as wide as possible. You might wish to look into a mirror to see if you have formed wrinkles on the forehead.
2. Tense the muscles on either side of your nose as if you were going to sneeze.
3. Dilate or flare out your nostrils.
4. Force an extended smile from "ear to ear" while at the same time clenching your teeth.
5. Pull one corner of your mouth up and then the other up as in a "villainous sneer."
6. Draw your chin up as close to your chest as possible.
7. Do the opposite of the above, trying to draw your head back as close to your back as possible.

Muscles of the Trunk

Included in this group are the muscles of the back, chest, abdomen, and pelvis. Here are ways you can tense these muscles.

1. Bring your chest forward and at the same time put your shoulder back, with emphasis on bringing your shoulder blades as close together as possible.
2. Try to round your shoulders and bring your shoulder blades far apart. This is basically the opposite of the above.
3. Give your shoulders a shrug, trying to bring them up to your ears as you simultaneously try to bring your neck downward.
4. Breathe deeply and hold it momentarily and then blow out the air from your lungs rapidly.
5. Draw in your stomach muscles so that your chest is out beyond your stomach. Exert your stomach muscles by forcing out to make it look as if your stomach protrudes more than it does.

Muscles of the Upper Extremities

This group includes muscles of the hands, forearms, upper arms, and shoulders. A number of muscles situated in the trunk may be grouped with the muscles of the upper extremities, their function being to attach the upper limbs to the trunk and move the shoulders and arms. Some overlapping occurs in muscle groups *two* and *three*. Following are ways to tense these muscles.

1. Clench the fist and then open the hand, extending the fingers as far as possible.
2. Raise one arm shoulder high and parallel to the floor. Bend at the elbow and bring the hand in toward the shoulder. Try to touch your shoulders while attempting to move the shoulder away from the hand. Flex your opposite biceps in the same manner.
3. Stretch one arm out to the side of the body and try to point the fingers backward toward the body. Do the same with the other arm.
4. Hold the arm out the same way as in number two but this time have the palm facing up and point the fingers inward toward the body. Do the same with the other arm.
5. Stretch one arm out to the side, clench the fist, and roll the wrist around slowly. Do the same with the other arm.

Muscles of the Lower Extremities

This group includes muscles of the hips, thighs, legs, feet, and buttocks. Following are ways to tense some of these muscles.

1. Hold one leg out straight and point your toes as far forward as you can. Do the same with the other leg.
2. Follow the directions for number one, but point your toes as far backward as you can.
3. Turn each foot outward as far as you can and release. Do just the opposite by turning the foot inward as far as you can.
4. Try to draw the thigh muscles up so that you can see the form of the muscles.
5. Make your buttocks tense by pushing down if you are sitting in a chair. If you are lying down, try to draw the muscles of the buttocks in close by tensing.

These suggestions include several possibilities for tensing various muscles of the body. As you practice some of these, you will also discover other ways to tense and then let go. In the early stages, be alert to the possibility of cramping certain muscles. This can happen, particularly with those muscles that are not frequently used. Proceed carefully at the beginning. It might be a good idea to keep a record or diary of your sessions so that you can refer to these experiences if necessary. This also will help you begin each new session by reviewing your experiences in previous sessions.

USING RELAXATION WITH CHILDREN

For many years relaxation as a means of reducing stress was used only with adults. However, in more modern times relaxation procedures have been found to be very effective with children.

Relaxation training has been applied to problems involving cross-situational, overt motor behaviors of children, such as impulsivity, aggressiveness, and overactivity. The clearest applications have been made with hyperactive children, but relaxation training also has been applied to general aggression and learning problems.

The studies using relaxation training with hyperactive children have generally indicated that following training a reduction occurs in muscle tension, and ratings of behavior by parents improve when compared to hyperactive controls. On the surface, this could suggest that such training may be an effective treatment for hyperactivity. However, relaxation training has not yet been proven to be superior to other treatment alternatives. Conclusions regarding the findings in this area are limited by methodological and design flaws, including nonhomogeneous population sampling, inadequate numbers of subjects, and lack of adequate or appropriate control groups or conditions. Some factors during relaxation produce changes in the behavior of hyperactive children. However, the research to date does not appear to clearly indicate what these factors are.

Similar to the rationale for hyperactivity, relaxation training has been used to treat various learning and aggression problems. It is assumed that children who are tense or upset and who lack self-control have difficulty attending to learning tasks, and may be more likely to respond with aggression toward others when frustrated or provoked than nontense children with better self-control. Children who are taught to relax are believed to become much more amenable to learning alternative behaviors of new information.

The results of the application of relaxation training to children with learning problems and aggressive behavior are mixed. Some studies demonstrate positive effects over controls, while others show no difference between trained subjects and controls. In no instance does relaxation training result in behavior that was worse than that of a control group, so the application of relaxation training to these problem areas does not seem to represent a risk to subjects. In these studies, multiple sessions of relaxation training are used, strengthening the contention in the literature about adults that repeated training is necessary for acquisition of the relaxation skill and generalization of the skill to the academic environment.

As far as relaxation and avoidance behavior is concerned, the constructs of anxiety and fear can best be understood as physiological, cognitive, or behavioral arousal which functions to have the person avoid engaging in an aversive activity or coming into contact with an aversive stimulus. Relaxation training has long been applied to these problems under the assumption that relaxation serves as a competing response to the undesired arousal. In addition, relaxation may also facilitate the performance of a more adaptive behavior in a stressful situation.

The literature on using relaxation to reduce avoidance behavior is fairly consistent. Motor behavior is clearly reduced following relaxation training, but consistent cognitive and physiological changes are not always found. Studies that include multiple-relaxation procedures appear to affect multiple-arousal dimensions. Those that test muscle relaxation only demonstrate clear, consistent, satisfactory effects with overt behavioral measures. The mechanisms that are responsible for these differences are not yet identifiable, due to the lack of multiple, convergent measurement and comparisons of different relaxation training components.

Relaxation training has been increasingly applied to medical problems that are thought to be the result of or maintained by specific tension or physiological arousal. As such, relaxation is considered a primary treatment used to target a specific kind of medical problem. Similar to the way medication is used to target a particular physical symptom, relaxation training focuses on a particular response; the subject is taught to use the skill when the antecedent conditions related to the specific problems occur.

In general, applications of relaxation training to medical problems of children seems promising. With few exceptions, the results in this area indicate that relaxation training results in symptom improvement for asthma, headaches, seizures, and insomnia, although the clinical significance of these improvements is unclear. It is quite possible that different training procedures may be needed to impact the different problems presented in a medical setting. The remaining discussions in this chapter are concerned with forms of relaxation for specific use with children.

Creative Relaxation

The creative-relaxation approach suggested here combines a form of imagery and tensing and releasing. One person or a group creates a movement(s) designed to tense and relax individual muscles, muscle groups, or the entire body.

Creative relaxation simply means that there are contrasting creative movements that give the effect of tensing and letting go. An illustration is provided here for a better understanding of the concept.

This example shows the contrast (tensing and letting go) of the muscles of an upper extremity (arm). The leader could start by raising the following question: "What would you say is the main difference between a baseball bat and a jump rope?"

This question is then discussed and will no doubt lead to the major difference being that a baseball bat is hard and stiff and that a jump rope is soft and limp. The leader might then proceed as follows: "Let's see if we can make one of our arms be like a baseball bat." (This movement is created.) "Now, quickly, can you make your arm like a jump rope?" (The movement is created by releasing the tensed arm.)

The experience can be evaluated by using these questions: "How did your arm feel when you made it like a baseball bat?" "How did your arm feel when you made it like a jump rope?"

The creative person can produce a discussion that will increase an understanding of the relaxation phenomenon. This is but one example and one is limited only by imagination in developing others.

The Game Format for Practicing Relaxation

A game format can be used as a means of providing satisfactory relaxation. One advantage of this is that it can become more of a fun-oriented situation, avoiding the boredom that can result when using structured procedures. An example of the successful use of the game format is in the tensing and releasing phase with the game Simon Says. Each muscle group to be tensed and then relaxed is prefaced by "Simon says." "Simon says to close your eyes . . . . Simon says to make your eyebrows touch your hair . . . . Simon says to let go and feel your eyes relax." A four- or five-second tensing of any muscle is followed by an eight- to ten-second relaxing of the muscle. The sequence for relaxing the muscle prefaced by "Simon says" is as follows:

1. Head
   a. Try to make your eyebrows touch your hair.
   b. Squeeze your eyes shut.
   c. Wrinkle your nose.
   d. Press your lips together.
   e. Press your tongue against the roof of your mouth.

2. Shoulders and back
   a. Lift your shoulders and try to touch your ears.
   b. Bring your shoulders as far back as they will go.
3. Hands and arms
   a. Make your fist as tight as you can.
   b. Show me your arm muscles.
4. Stomach
   a. Make your stomach as hard as you can; pull it way in.
5. Upper legs
   a. Lift your legs and feet off the floor.
   b. Press your knees together.
6. Lower legs and feet.
   a. Press your ankles together.
   b. Press your feet together against the floor.

If a command is without the prefix "Simon says," the players remain motionless. For example, when the leader issues the command, "Simon says press your ankles together," everyone does this; but if the person playing Simon says, "Press your knees together," the players do not execute the command.

Mental Practice and Imagery

Mental practice is a symbolic rehearsal of a physical activity in the absence of any gross muscle movement. This means that a person imagines in his or her own mind the way to perform a given activity. *Imagery* is concerned with the development of a mental image that may aid one in the performance of an activity. In mental practice, the person thinks through what he or she is going to do, and with imagery may suggest, or another may suggest a condition, and he or she then tries to effect a mental image of the condition.

The use of mental practice in performing motor skills is not new. In fact, research in this general area has been going on for well over fifty years. This research has revealed that imagining a movement will likely produce recordable electric action potentials emanating from the muscle groups that would be called upon if the movement were to be actually carried out. In addition, most mental activity is accompanied by general rises in muscular tension.

One procedure in the use of mental practice for relaxation is that of making suggestions to oneself. For the most part, in early childhood, we first learn to act on the basis of verbal instructions from others. Later we begin to guide and direct our own behavior on the basis of our own language activities—we literally talk to ourselves, giving ourselves instructions. This point of view has long been supported by research that postulates that speech as a form of communication between children and adults later becomes a means of organizing the child's own behavior. That is, the function that was previously divided between two people—child and adult—becomes an internal function of human behavior. Following is an example of this approach.

> I am going to relax completely. First, I will relax my forehead and scalp. I will let all of the muscles of my forehead and scalp relax and become completely at rest. All of the wrinkles will come out of my forehead and that part of my body will relax completely. Now, I will relax the muscles of my face. (Continue the procedure from head to toe.)

Imagery can be used to promote a relaxed state by making *comparative* statements such as "float like a feather," or "melt like ice." Creative persons will be able to think of many such comparative statements to assist in producing a relaxed state.

Another way imagery can be used to promote a relaxed state is the use of the following stories that I have prepared for this purpose. The adult reads the story to the child, and then with various degrees of adult guidance, the child tries to depict the activity in the reading selection by creating his or her own responses that facilitate relaxation.

> *Snowflakes*
> Snow!
> Snowflakes fall.
> They fall down.
> Down, down, down.
> Around and around.
> Could you move like snowflakes?

> *Mr. Snowman and Mr. Sun*
> See Mr. Snowman.
> See Mr. Sun.
> Mr. Snowman sees Mr. Sun.
> Mr. Snowman is going.
> Going, going, going.
> Mr. Snowman is gone.
> Be Mr. Snowman.

Creative adults should be able to develop their own stories. The following guidelines are submitted for this purpose: In general, words that are new to the child should be used sparingly. Repetition of words is encouraged. Sentence length and lack of complexity in sentences should be considered in keeping the level of difficulty of material within the child's independent reading level.

Finally, it bears repeating that relaxation is a skill that must be learned. This means that one cannot necessarily expect immediate positive results. However, with practice the skill can be accomplished to the extent that it will serve as an excellent procedure for reducing stress in children.

Chapter 11

Reducing Stress Through Meditation

The art of meditation dates back more than 2,000 years. Until recent times, this ancient art has been associated with religious as well as cultural connotations. In the 1960s, countercultures began using it as a route to a more natural means of living and relaxing. Today, people from all walks of life practice and realize the positive effects that meditation can have upon the human mind and body.

It is difficult to determine precisely how many people practice meditation. My own studies show that, in most populations, about 4 or 5 percent use meditation as a stress-reducing technique. One exception to this is its use among psychiatrists, with about 20 percent of them reporting that they engage in meditation to reduce stress. It should not be surprising that physicians who specialize in disorders of the mind would themselves practice this technique more than others. As mentioned in Chapter 10, the theory of meditation is that if the mind is quieted, then other systems of the body will tend to be stabilized more readily.

Kenneth Pelletier[1] asserted that meditation should be defined as an experimental exercise involving an individual's actual attention, not belief systems or other cognitive processes, and that it should not be confused with prolonged, self-induced lethargy. The nervous system needs intensity and variety of external stimulation to maintain proper functioning.

Robert Woolfolk and Frank Richardson[2] suggest that at the very least meditation can give the mind a rest—a brief vacation from stress and worry, one that requires neither a travel agent nor days free from the responsibility of work or family. It is almost as though meditation allows us to temporarily shut down those information-processing mechanisms of the brain that are ultimately responsible for producing stress. In addition, meditation can give us a more balanced outlook and increased energy for dealing with whatever difficulties we face.

Although there are many meditation techniques, *concentration* is an important factor contributing to success in most of them. The mind's natural flow from one idea to another is quieted by the individual's concentration. Lowering mental activity may be an easy task, but almost total elimination of scattered thoughts takes a great deal of time and practice on the part of the meditator.

The question sometimes raised is: Are sleep and meditation the same thing? Sleep has been linked to meditation, as both are hypometabolic states, that is, restful states where the body experiences decreased metabolism. But meditation is not a form of sleep. Although some similar psychological changes have been found in sleep and meditation, they are not the same and one is not a substitute for the other. Various studies have shown that meditation may restore more energy than sleep does.

Countless positive pronouncements about meditation come from some of the most notable scientists of modern times, who spend a good proportion of their time studying stress. However, only in recent years has the scientific community uncovered many of the positive effects that repeated meditation has upon stress-ridden individuals. Various scientific studies have shown that meditation can actually decrease the possibility of an individual contracting stress-related disorders, and that meditators have a much faster recovery rate than nonmeditators when exposed to a stressful situation. Specifically from a physiological point of view, meditation decreases the body's metabolic rate, which involves decreases in the following bodily functions:

1. oxygen consumption,
2. breathing rate,
3. heart rate and blood pressure,
4. sympathetic nervous system activity, and
5. blood lactate (a chemical produced in the body during stressful encounters).

Also, meditation tends to increase the psychological ability and reduce anxiety in those who practice it. Research seems to be disclosing that meditation can be a path to better health.

TYPES OF MEDITATION

Having conducted a rather thorough examination of the literature on meditation, I have been able to identify more than twenty meditational systems. Interestingly enough, one technique is about as good as another for improving the way we handle stress.

I have arbitrarily selected for discussion four types of meditation: (1) Christian meditation, (2) meditative running, (3) strategic meditation, and (4) Transcendental Meditation.

Christian Meditation

If you ask the average person about meditation the response will ordinarily be that it primarily involves "sitting and thinking," or "engaging in silent prayer." Basically, this is what Christian meditation is. One feels that he or she is meditating by reflecting upon certain experiences and evaluating certain activities that have taken place in one's life.

Meditative Running

Two prominent researchers, Diane Hales and Robert Hales,[3] have reported on a concept regarding a combination of meditation and running, what I would describe as meditative running. Although running and meditation seem like completely opposite states—one strenuous and the other serene—both can be considered as paths to altered states of consciousness, and together they can profoundly affect both body and mind. Exercisers who meditate as they work out literally change the way their hearts and lungs function. They burn less oxygen and use energy more efficiently.

Strategic Meditation

Amarjit S. Sethi,[4] has developed a concept called strategic meditation. He defines it as a process of balancing "calculative thinking" and "noncalculative thinking." In order to give specificity to this concept he has labeled it strategic meditation so that it may be distinguished from other forms of meditation. The meditational process takes place in different contexts, comprising both the facts and the values of a given environment. The study of interactions between facts and values in shaping calculative and noncalculative thinking becomes a process of strategic meditation. It is strategic because meditation examines problems, identifies their nature, and establishes perspective. It is meditational because a person transforms the problem-solving orientation through a focus on both the problem and its solution, and this begins to suggest elements of how an individual processes information in a relatively "problem-solving free context" which has been termed noncalculative. Another term for this level of consciousness is *playfulness*. The emphasis in a meditational exercise shifts from complex calculation and sophisticated decision rules to selective perception. This leads to a problem-free context.

In order to practice strategic meditation one needs to develop his or her own diagnosis of the problem. Problem solving is utilized as a process of investigating the source of stress and is integrated as a part of the meditational process. This phase involves perception of the environment, analysis of the problem, and design of alternative solutions. The problem-solving process is integrated with a meditational process.

Transcendental Meditation

Of the various types of meditation, Transcendental Meditation (TM) is by far the best known. It was introduced in the United States in the 1960s by Maharishi Mahesh Yogi. It is believed that he used the term transcendental (a literal meaning of which is "going beyond") to indicate that the process projects one beyond the level of a wakeful experience to a state of profound rest along with heightened alertness.[5]

TM involves the repetition of a mantra (a word or specific sound) for fifteen to twenty minutes daily with the meditator in a relaxed position with eyes closed. Almost without exception, those who practiced TM attest to its positive effects. Although other forms of meditation may involve specific procedures, it is safe to say that most derive in some way from basic TM. The discussion that follows is based on this type of meditation.

A PROCEDURE FOR MEDITATING

Presented here is a description of a procedure for meditating that has been found to be successful. Many of my students have reported successful results from its use. However, meditation is an individual matter, and what may be beneficial for one person may not necessarily be so for another.

Certain basic considerations should be taken into account when beginning a meditation program. The following descriptive list of these considerations is general in nature, and the reader can alter the suggestions to fit individual needs and interests.

1. *Locate a quiet place and assume a comfortable position.* The importance of a quiet environment should be obvious since concentration is facilitated in a tranquil surrounding. The position one assumes for meditation is an individual matter. However, when it is suggested that one assume a comfortable position, this might be amended by, "but not too comfortable." If one is too comfortable there is the possibility of falling asleep, and this, of course, would defeat the purpose of meditation. For this reason, one should consider an upright position while meditating.

   A position might be taken to include some latitude for swaying. This can provide for a comfortable posture and, at the same time, guard against falling asleep. The person must be in a comfortable enough position to remain this way for fifteen minutes or so. One such position might be sitting on the floor with legs crossed, back straight, and resting on the legs and buttocks. The head should be erect and the hands resting in the lap. If you prefer to sit in a chair rather than on the floor, select a chair with a straight back. You need to be the judge of comfort, and, thus, you should select a position where you feel you are able to concentrate and remain in this position for a period of time.

2. *Focus your concentration.* As mentioned previously, concentration is essential to successful meditation. If you focus on one specific factor, such as an object, sound, or personal feeling, it is less likely that your thoughts will be distracted. Consider focusing on a fantasy trip, reexperiencing a trip already taken, a place that has not been visited, or a certain sound or chant.

3. *Use a nonsense word or phrase.* Some techniques of meditation, such as the popular TM, involve the chanting of a particular word (mantra) as one meditates. Although the mantra has important meaning for the meditator, I refer to it as a nonsense word because it should be devoid of any connotation that would send one thinking in many directions. This, of course, would hinder concentration, so a nonsense word should perhaps be most effective. Incidentally, I have found in my own experience with meditation that the practice of chanting such a word is very effective.

4. *Be aware of natural breathing rhythm.* The importance of natural breathing rhythm should not be underestimated. In fact, some clinical psychologists recommend this as a means of concentrating. One can count the number of times he or she inhales, and this in itself is a relaxing mental activity.

5. *The time for meditation.* Since meditation is an activity to quiet the mind, it is strongly recommended that the practice not be undertaken immediately at the end of the day. At this time, the mind may be in a very active state of reviewing the day's activities. My own personal experience suggests a fifteen- to twenty-minute period in the morning and another such period in the evening, preferably before dinner, or possibly two hours after dinner.

With these considerations in mind, you should be ready to experiment. To begin, assume a comfortable position in a quiet place in as passive an environment as possible. Try to dismiss all wandering thoughts from your mind and concentrate on a relaxed body while keeping the eyes closed. When feeling fairly relaxed, the repetition of the nonsense word or phrase can begin. This can be repeated orally or silently. Personally, I have had good success repeating it silently, that is, through the mind. Repeat your chosen word or phrase in this manner over and over, keeping the mind clear of any passing thoughts. At first, this may be very difficult, but with practice it becomes easier.

After fifteen to twenty minutes have passed (or less if you wish), discontinue repetition of the word or phrase. Become aware of your relaxed body once again. Give yourself a few moments before moving as your body will need to readjust. For successful, prolonged results one might consider continuing the practice two times daily for fifteen- to twenty-minute sessions.

If you have difficulty trying to meditate on your own, seek the services of an experienced meditator for assistance and supervision. The recent growing popularity of meditation has been accomplished by the establishment of instructional meditation centers in some communities.

USING MEDITATION WITH CHILDREN

Evidence exists that supports the practice of meditation as beneficial for children. All family members can learn meditation techniques, and children as young as ten years of age can learn, although they should meditate for less than fifteen minutes. Often, younger children become interested in learning to meditate after others in the family have begun practicing the technique.

In some cases, courses in the technique of Transcendental Meditation have been prepared for elementary school children and implemented by some teachers. Among other things, this type of program improves creativity. Perhaps child psychologists should investigate the effect of the children's technique of TM on early development and creativity.

A great deal of research on meditation for children has appeared in the literature over the years, and contrary to general opinion, this is not a recent innovation. In this regard, I am presenting some of the findings of the early work in this area.

With regard to creativity, Gowan[6] studied the facilitation of creativity through meditation. He reviewed the emerging concepts of creativity along with therapeutic procedures designed to relieve the mental blocks caused by anxiety and stress. He found that various studies using TM increased creativity, decreased anxiety, and controlled stress. The results of these studies have suggested that children could be helped to obtain greater creativity through knowledge of one or more meditation techniques.

Early work by Rozman,[7] based on actual experience in teaching the science of meditation to children three to thirteen years of age, has been shown to help make group work with children peaceful, integrated, and meaningful. In addition, meditation assists children in resolving personal problems and stresses. Moreover, Rozman found that meditation can be used successfully with gifted, mentally retarded, and average or hyperactive children.

Some very interesting research has been done with regard to attentiveness of children. Murdock[8] describes an approach used by an elementary school teacher who taught meditation exercises to a class of twenty-five normal and highly gifted kindergarten children. Breathing exercises and tensing and loosening of muscles were used before going into the meditation process. Feedback from children themselves seemed to suggest increased levels of attention span.

In another study involving attention, Redfering[9] had eighteen children, eight to eleven years old, participate in either the treatment group and practice Herbert Benson's meditative-relaxation technique or, in the nontreatment group, relaxing for the same twenty-minute sessions over a five-day period. Nonattending (meaning not paying attention) behavioral levels were recorded during the treatment period. Mean change differences of nonattending behaviors for the two groups reflected a significant reduction in the number of nonattending behaviors for the treatment group.

Kratter and Hogan[10] conducted a study regarding attention deficit disorder with hyperactivity. A total of twenty-four children, meeting several criteria for being diagnosed as having attention deficit disorder with hyperactivity, were selected for the study. Children were assigned to one of three categories: a meditation-training group, a progressive-muscle relaxation group, or a waiting-list group. Subjects in the training groups were seen on an individual basis for twenty minutes twice weekly for a period of four weeks. Meditating subjects sat with eyes closed, breathed slowly and deeply and repeated the Sanskrit word *ahnam* ("nameless") first aloud and then silently for periods gradually increasing in duration from two to eight minutes. Progressive-muscle relaxing subjects tensed and relaxed hands, forearms, biceps, triceps, shoulders, stomach, thighs, and calves in periods increasing from two to eight minutes. Results indicated that both the meditation-training and relaxation-training groups showed significant decreases in levels of impulsivity. No change in impulsivity was found in the control group. In the measures of selective deployment of attention and freedom from distractibility, only meditation training resulted in a significant improvement in the behavior of children in both the meditation-training and relaxation-training groups. Parent rating scales reflected a significant improvement in the behavior of children in both the meditation-training and relaxation-training groups.

In the field of special education, Ferguson[11] reviewed research on the physiological, perceptual, and psychological benefits of TM for potential applicability to exceptional children. Meditation was perceived as important to education, in that it is reported to improve learning, memory, grades, interpersonal relationships, and cognitive-perceptual functioning. It was suggested that meditation would be applicable to exceptional *or* developmentally disabled children.

The studies reported here comprise but a few of the large number that have been undertaken in the area of effectiveness of meditation for children. In most cases, these examples have shown a very positive effect of meditation. However, certain precautions need to be taken into account when interpreting the results, and the reader is reminded of possible limitations.

Choosing meditation as a technique for stress reduction is an individual matter. I reported previously that a relatively small number of those in my surveys used meditation as a means of coping with stress; however, all of the respondents who do utilize it reported great success and recommend it for others.

Chapter 12

Reducing Stress Through Biofeedback

When discussing biofeedback, we are dealing with a complex and complicated subject. This phenomenon will be discussed in terms of what it is supposed to be and what it is supposed to do. In the early stages of biofeedback training (BFT), it should take place under qualified supervision. This means that anyone wishing to pursue an interest in, and eventually participate in BFT, should seek the services of one trained in this area.

THE MEANING OF BIOFEEDBACK

The term *feedback* has been used in various frames of reference. It may have been used originally in engineering in connection with control systems that involve feedback procedures. These feedback control systems make adjustments to environmental changes, such as in the case of a thermostat controlling temperature levels in the home. According to Barbara Brown,[1] one of the foremost early authorities on the subject of biofeedback, the terms *feedback* and *control systems* were borrowed by physiologists when they began theorizing about how the functions of the body were performed.

Learning theorists use the term feedback interchangeably with the expression *knowledge of results* to describe the process of providing the learner information as to how accurate his or her reactions were. In other words, feedback is knowledge of various kinds that the performer receives about his or her performance. With particular reference to motor-skill learning, feedback in the form of knowledge of results is the strongest, most important variable controlling performance and learning. Furthermore, studies have repeatedly shown that there is no improvement without it, progressive improvement with it, and deterioration after its withdrawal.

Biofeedback can be described in numerous ways. It is any information that we receive about the functioning of our internal organs such as the heart, sweat glands, muscles, and brain. Another description indicates that it is a process in which information about our organism's biologic activity is supplied for perception by the same organism. This could be extended by indicating that biofeedback is the monitoring of signals from the body, such as muscle tension and hand warmth, and the feeding of this information back through the use of sophisticated machines to individuals so they can get external information as to exactly what is happening in their bodies.

Many individual feedback systems exist in the human body. The five senses perceive information about the external environment and relay it to a control center, usually the brain, where it is integrated with other relevant information. When the sensed information is significant enough, central control generates commands for appropriate body changes.

These senses can also be thought of as the systems of *perception,* that is, how we obtain information from the environment and what we make of it. Learning theorists agree that the forms of perception most involved in learning are *auditory* perception, *visual* perception, *kinesthetic* perception, and *tactile* perception. Auditory perception is the mental interpretation of what a person hears. Visual perception is the mental interpretation of what a person sees. Kinesthetic perception is the mental interpretation of the sensation of body movement. Tactile perception is the mental interpretation of what a person experiences through the sense of touch. In this regard, it is common practice among learning theorists to refer to auditory feedback, visual feedback, kinesthetic feedback, and tactile feedback.

BIOFEEDBACK INSTRUMENTATION

We are all aware of the fact that the human body itself is a complicated and complex biofeedback instrument, which alerts us to certain internal activity, as mentioned in the previous discussion. However, many researchers believe a need still exists for sensitive instruments to monitor physiological and psychological reactivity. Following is a brief discussion of the more widely known biofeedback instruments that are used both for research and therapeutic purposes.

Electromyograph (EMG)

Electromyography is the recording of electric phenomena occurring in muscles during contraction. Needle or skin electrodes are used and connected with an oscilloscope so that action potentials may be viewed and recorded (the oscilloscope is an instrument that visually displays an electrical wave on a fluorescent screen). Before electromyography was available, guesswork ordinarily had to be used to try to determine the participation of the muscles in movement. When a muscle is completely relaxed or inactive, it has no electric potential; however, when it is engaged in contraction, current appears.

It is believed that EMG training can produce deep muscle relaxation and relieve tension. A person gets the feedback by seeing a dial or hearing a sound from a machine and he or she knows immediately the extent of which certain muscles may be relaxed or tensed. A muscle frequently used in EMG training for research and other purposes is the frontalis, located in the front of the head.

Feedback Thermometers

The obvious purpose of feedback thermometers is to record body temperatures. Ordinarily, a thermistor is attached to the hands or fingers. This highly sensitive instrument shows very small increments of degrees of temperature change; the person receives the information with a visual or auditory signal. This feedback instrumentation has been recommended for reduction of stress and anxiety and autonomic nervous system relaxation.

Electroencephalograph (EEG)

The purpose of the electroencephalograph is to record amplitude and frequency of brain waves, and it has been used in research for many years. It has also been used with success to diagnose certain clinical diseases. In addition, EEG feedback has been used in psychotherapy and in reducing stress and pain.

An interesting relatively recent horizon for EEG feedback is how it might be involved in creativity and learning. In fact, some individuals who are creative have indicated that they can emerge from the EEG theta rhythm state (high-amplitude brain-wave pattern) with answers to problems that they were previously unable to solve. The theta waves are ordinarily recorded when a person is in a state of drowsiness or is actually falling asleep. It is perhaps for this reason that some refer to this condition as "sleep learning." Since it is a state just before sleep, others refer to it as the twilight period of "twilight learning."

Galvanic Skin Response (GSR)

Several different kinds of GSR instruments are used to measure changes in electrical resistance of the skin to detect emotional arousal. The instrument reacts in proportion to the amount of perspiration one emits and the person is informed of the changes in electrical resistance by an auditory or visual signal. One form of GSR test is the polygraph, or lie detector, which is supposed to record a physiological response associated with lying. GSR feedback is often recommended for use of relaxation, reducing tension, improvement of ability to sleep, or for emotional control.

In general, the purpose of the biofeedback machinery is to provide accurate and reliable data that will increase one's awareness of how the body is functioning and demonstrate one's influence over his or her action of the body. This information should be useful in inspiring a person to take an active self-interest in his or her own well-being. After such information is received, if it has been obtained under the supervision of a qualified person, there may be a given number of sessions arranged for consultation and training. Perhaps the ultimate objective is for the individual to be able to gain control over his or her own autonomic nervous system.

As popular and well-advertised as biofeedback machinery has become, it is not without its critics who feel that many important purposes can be accomplished without instruments by using the body as its own biofeedback instrument. In general, they identify such factors as:

1. diverse muscle relaxation,
2. change of heart rate and body temperature,
3. change of breathing patterns,
4. decrease of stress and anxiety reactions,
5. mental relaxation,
6. autonomic nervous system relaxation,

7. pain relief for tension headaches, backaches, and other aches and pains, and
8. improved learning ability, including enhancement of concentration and recall.

However, the critics would probably admit that certain biofeedback instruments, particularly EMG, have important applications for retraining of patients following disease and injury.

It is difficult to determine unequivocally what the future of biofeedback may be. Without question, it has influenced our way of thinking with reference to a person being able to possibly control his or her physiological functions. In view of this, perhaps one of its foremost contributions is that it creates in an individual a feeling of responsibility for his or her personal well-being.

USING BIOFEEDBACK WITH CHILDREN

Biofeedback has been used with considerable success with children, and research in this area has increased appreciably in recent years. However, as in the case of meditation, there is little awareness of the extent of this research and how long it has been conducted. Some of the early research on biofeedback with children is presented here.

Biofeedback for children has been used both in the clinical and school settings; however, it has found more prevalent use in the former and it is in this setting that most research has been undertaken.

Among the prominent researchers are two of my former collaborators, Carter and Russell.[2] They conducted a study which included eleven treatment combinations and three age ranges with a total of 132 subjects, 114 of whom completed the program. Each student received his randomly assigned treatment combination two times per week for six weeks. The four individual treatments were: (1) EMG biofeedback for twenty minutes each time, (2) handwriting practice, (3) prerecorded relaxation tapes, and (4) homework with prerecorded audiotapes. They were given a comprehensive battery, including the Slosson Intelligence Test, one week before and one week after treatment. They found that listening to prerecorded relaxation tapes was the best predictor of gains in reading comprehension, and that biofeedback training significantly enhanced the predictability of gains in reading comprehension. In fact, the children who received biofeedback and heard the tapes showed significant change in ten of the eleven measures. The change was maintained or improved over time (ten-month follow-up). Children who did not receive the treatments showed improvement only on one of eleven variables and the follow-up scores tended to decrease slightly if not significantly. Significant improvements were obtained in verbal IQ, reading, spelling, arithmetic computation, auditory memory, eye-hand coordination, and written expression.

Houts[3] administered three weeks of relaxation training followed by weekly thermal biofeedback sessions to an eleven-year-old boy who had suffered severe headaches since he was six years old. The boy's headache frequency was greatly reduced. A one-year follow-up revealed that headache frequency remained negligible. Results suggested that child migraine may be amenable to procedures reported to be effective with adult migraine.

Omizo and associates[4] examined effects of EMG biofeedback and relaxation training on memory task performance by hyperactive nine- to eleven-year-old boys. Forty-eight subjects were identified through teachers' ratings on the Conners' Behavior Rating Scale-Abbreviated Form and divided into experimental and control groups. Experimental treatment consisted of three two-phase (biofeedback and relaxation training) EMG sessions. Controls' EMG equipment was inoperative so they did not receive biofeedback or relaxation training. Subjects completed pre- and posttreatment memory tasks—a paired associate word list (the Dolch Basic Memory List) and picture—recall tasks (the Peabody Picture Vocabulary Test (PPVT). Results showed that experimental subjects performed better on the paired associate test and achieved better muscle relaxation than controls. Performance on the PPVT did not prove to be significantly different for experimental and control groups when effects of post-EMG recordings and performance on the paired associate word list were controlled for, although univariate F values and multiple analysis of variance procedures revealed significant differences between groups on all variables examined.

Three boys aged nine to eleven years meeting multiple criteria for hyperactivity were trained by Raymer and Poppen[5] to emit ten specific relaxed behaviors by means of behavioral relaxation training

(BRT). Dependent measures included a behavioral relaxation scale, frontalis EMG, parent symptom questionnaire, and self-reports. A multiple-probe design across subjects was employed, plus a switch between recliner and beanbag chair for each subject. BRT was effective in producing high levels of relaxed behaviors and low EMG levels in the office setting, particularly in conjunction with the beanbag chair, with some reduction on hyperactivity scores on the parent questionnaire. Subsequent training in each child's home by his mother was accomplished by further reductions in parent-reported symptoms and low EMG levels, which were maintained at a one-month follow-up.

Karnes, Oehler, and Jones[6] investigated the relationship between biofeedback and tension, as measured by an EMG and Children's Personality Questionnaire (CPQ), in thirty-seven intellectually gifted fourth- to seventh-graders. Results showed that indirect factors which measure tension on the CPQ were correlated significantly with biofeedback measures. Those subjects who became the most relaxed during biofeedback training appeared to be the least tense on the CPQ. Contrary to these findings, the relaxed-tense factor of the CPQ was correlated significantly and negatively with biofeedback measures, which indicated that the subjects may not have been aware of their own tense state and thus would benefit from biofeedback training.

In the final study reported here involving the effect of frontal EMG biofeedback training on the behavior of children with activity-level problems, Hughes, Henry, and Hughes[7] employed N=1 withdrawal designs with three children with such problems. Tutoring sessions occurred daily over a two and one-half month period. Each child was reinforced for decreasing frontalis muscle tension during auditory feedback while working arithmetic problems. Feedback was faded while tension reduction was maintained. These procedures were repeated with reinforcement for increasing, rather than decreasing, muscle tension. Frontal EMG level, percent of time on task, and motoric activity rate were obtained during sessions. Parent ratings of problem behavior in the home were recorded daily. Biofeedback with reinforcement was effective in both raising and lowering muscle tension. Effects were maintained by reinforcement. Results suggested a direct relationship between tension and activity levels. Academic performance improved and problem behavior decreased significantly with reductions in EMG activity, although individual exceptions to these findings were present. Results lend support to the efficacy of frontal EMG biofeedback training in reducing activity, increasing attention to an academic task, and reducing problem behaviors.

In concluding this chapter, it is worth repeating that, at least in the early stages, the practice of biofeedback training should take place under the supervision of a qualified person. In addition, if a disease syndrome is present a physician's referral may be required. Finally, all of the stress-reduction techniques referred to throughout this book have met with various degrees of success when applied in the appropriate manner.

Notes

Chapter 1

1. Selye, Hans, *Stress Without Distress*. New York: New American Library, 1975, p. 17.
2. Walker, C. Eugene, *Learn to Relax: 13 Ways to Reduce Tension*. Englewood Cliffs, NJ: Prentice-Hall, Inc., 1975, p. 16.
3. Viscott, David, *The Language of Feelings*. New York: Arbor House, 1976, p. 93.
4. Thomas, William C., Avoiding Burnout: Hardiness As a Buffer in College Athletes. Reston, VA. *Research Quarterly for Exercise and Sport,* 69 Supplement, 1998, p. 116.
5. Small, Gary, *The Memory Bible*. New York: Hyperion, 2002, p. 77.

Chapter 2

1. Selye, Hans, *Stress Without Distress*. New York: New American Library, 1975, p. 17.
2. Cannon, Walter B., *The Wisdom of the Body*. New York: W.W. Norton, 1932, p. 23.
3. Posner, Israel and Leitner, Lewis, Eustress vs. Distress: Determination by Predictability and Controllability of the Stressor. *Stress, The Official Journal of the International Institute of Stress and Its Affiliates,* Summer 1981, p. 5.
4. Mikhail, Anis, Stress: A Psychological Connection. *The Journal of Human Stress,* June 1981, pp. 1, 33.
5. Holmes, T.H. and Rahe, R.H., The Social Readjustment Scale. *Journal of Psychosomatic Research,* November 1967, p. 12.
6. Lazarus, Richard, Little Hassles Can Be Hazardous to Your Health. *Psychology Today,* June 1981, p. 16.
7. Small Gary, *The Memory Bible*. New York: Hyperion, 2002, p. 64.
8. Bremner, J. Douglas, *Does Stress Damage the Brain? Understanding Trauma-Related Disorders from a Neurological Perspective*. New York: W.W. Norton, 2002, p. 12.
9. Yang, B. and Clum, G.A., Childhood Stress Leads to Later Suicidality Via Its Effect on Cognitive Functioning. *Suicide and Life-Threatening Behavior,* Fall 2000, p. 183.

Chapter 3

1. Zimmerman, Jean and Reavill, Gil, The Crying Game. *Working Woman,* March 2002, p. 54.
2. Small, Gary, *The Memory Bible.* New York, Hyperion, 2002, p. 66.

Chapter 5

1. Rosch, Paul J., Stress of Sex Abuse Weakens the Immune System. *Health and Stress* (Newsletter of the American Institute of Stress), 10, 1994, p. 6.
2. Gullotta, Thomas P., and Donohue, Karen D., Families, Relocation, and the Corporation. *New Directions for Mental Health Services,* December 1983, p. 15.
3. Godbey, Cathy, Mathematics Anxiety and the Undergraduate Student. *Research in Education,* June 1999, p. 89.

Chapter 6

1. Pelletier, Kenneth R., *Mind As Healer Mind As Slayer.* New York: Dell Publishing Company, 1977, p. 7.
2. Selye, Hans, *Stress Without Distress.* New York: New American Library, 1975, p. 24.
3. Piening, Suzanne, Family Stress in Diabetic Renal Failure. *Health and Social Work,* Spring 1984, p. 134.
4. Hollander, Jurgen and Florin, Irmela, Expressed Emotion and Airway Conductance in Children with Bronchial Asthma. *Journal of Psychosomatic Research,* April 1982, p. 307.
5. Barbarin, Oscar A. and Chesler, Mark A., Coping As an Interpersonal Strategy: Families with Childhood Cancer. *Family Systems Medicine,* Fall 1984, p. 279.
6. Gallagher, James H., Beckman, Paula, and Cross, Arthur H., Families of Handicapped Children: Sources of Stress and Its Amelioration. *Exceptional Children,* September 1983, p. 407.
7. Wikler, Lynn, Haack, Jane, and Intagliata, James, Bearing the Burden Alone: Helping Divorced Mothers of Children with Developmental Disabilities. *Family Therapy Collection,* November 1984, p. 44.
8. Greenberg, Mark T., Family Stress and Child Competence: The Effects of Early Intervention for Families with Deaf Infants. *American Annals of the Deaf,* June 1983, p. 407.
9. Crnic, Keith A., Friedrich, William N., and Greenberg, Mark T., Adaptation of Families with Mentally Retarded Children: A Model of Stress, Coping, and Family Ecology. *American Journal of Mental Deficiency,* September 1983, p. 125.
10. Seshadri, Mala, Impact of a Mentally Handicapped Child on the Family. *Indian Journal of Clinical Psychology,* September 1983, p. 473.
11. Klingman, Arigdor, Mass Innoculation in a Community: The Effect of Primary Prevention of Stress Reactions. *American Journal of Community,* June 1985, p. 323.

12. Dollinger, Stephen J., O'Donnell, James P., and Staley, Arlinda A. Lightning-Strike Disaster: Effects on Children's Fears and Worries. *Journal of Consulting and Clinical Psychology,* December 1984, p. 1028.

13. Ordway, Janet E., A Home Burns: Stress in a Family. *Psychiatric Journal of the University of Ottawa,* September 1984, p. 127.

14. Bassin, Donna T., Wolfe, Karen M., and Thier, Adrienne, Children's Reactions to Psychiatric Hospitalizataion: Drawings and Storytelling As a Database. *The Arts in Psychotherapy,* Spring 1983, p. 33.

15. Burgess, Ann W., Response Patterns in Children and Adolescents Exploited Through Sex Rings and Pornography. *American Journal of Psychiatry,* May 1984, p. 656.

Chapter 7

1. Small, Gary, *The Memory Bible.* New York: Hyperion, 2002, p. 158.

2. Brody, Jane, *Jane Brody's Nutrition Book.* New York: W.W. Norton and Company, 1981, p. 83.

3. Morse, Donald and Pollack, Robert, The Stress-Free Anti-Aging Diet, No. 3 in the series *Stress in Modern Society,* James H. Humphrey, Editor. New York: AMS Press, Inc., 1989, p. 129.

4. Palm, J. Daniel, *Diet Away Your Stress, Tension, and Anxiety.* New York: Doubleday and Co. Inc., 1976, p. 82.

5. Brownell, Kelly D. and Ludwig, David S., Fighting Obesity and the Food Lobby. *The Washington Post,* June 9, 2002, p. 21A.

6. Brown, David, Diabetic Children Suffer As Young Adults. *The Washington Post,* June 17, 2002, p. 19A.

Chapter 8

1. McQuade, Walter and Aikman, Ann, *Stress.* New York: E.P. Dutton and Co., 1974, p. 81.

2. Jencks, Beata, *Your Body Feedback at Its Best.* Chicago: Nelson-Hall, Inc., 1977, pp. 51, 172.

3. Walker, C. Eugene, *Learn to Relax: 13 Ways to Reduce Tension.* Englewood Cliffs, NJ: Prentice-Hall, Inc., 1975, p. 16.

4. Driscoll, Richard, Exertion Therapy. *Behavior Today,* April, 1975, p. 27.

Chapter 9

1. The Mysteries of Sleep Continue to Baffle Scientists. *Health,* September 9, 1997, p. 10.

2. Streitfield, David, And So to Bed . . . but Not Necessarily to Sleep. *Health,* April 21, 1988, p. 6.

3. Small, Gary, *The Memory Bible.* New York: Hyperion, 2002, p. 77.

4. Vedantane, Shanker, Do We Really Need to Sleep? And Why. *Health,* May 2002, p. 1.

5. Rosch, Paul, J., Memory and Brain Function. *Health and Stress* (Newsletter of the American Institute of Stress), 6, 1996, p. 3.

6. Rosch, Paul J., Sleep and Your Heart. *Health and Stress* (Newsletter of the American Institute of Stress), 6, 1996, p. 3.

7. Anthony, William A., *The Art of Napping.* Burdett, NY: Larson Publications, 1997.

8. Help Kids Earn A's in Bed. *Parade,* September 1, 2002, p. 10.

Chapter 10

1. Benson, Herbert, *The Relaxation Response.* New York: William Morrow and Company, Inc., 1975, p. 7.

2. Jacobson, Edmund, *You Must Relax,* Fourth Edition. New York: McGraw-Hill, 1962, p. 23.

Chapter 11

1. Pelletier, Kenneth, *Mind As Healer Mind As Slayer.* New York: Dell Publishing Co., 1977, p. 7.

2. Woolfolk, Robert L. and Richardson, Frank C., *Stress, Survival and Society.* New York: New American Library, 1981, p. 68.

3. Hales, Diane and Hales, Robert, Exercising the Psyche. *Health,* June 5, 1985, p. 3.

4. Sethi, Amarjit, Meditation As an Intervention in Stress Reactivity, No. 12 in the series on *Stress in Modern Society,* James H. Humphrey, Editor. New York: AMS Press, Inc., 1989, p. 16.

5. Bloomfield, Harold H., *TM: Discovering Inner Energy and Overcoming Stress.* Boston: G.K. Hall, 1976, p. 7.

6. Gowan, John, The Facilitation of Creativity Through Meditation Procedures. *Journal of Creative Behavior,* December 1976, p. 156.

7. Rozman, Deborah, *Meditating with Children: A Workbook on New Age Educational Methods.* Boulder Creek, CA: University of the Trees, 1976, p. 49.

8. Murdock, Maureen H., Meditation with Young Children. *Journal of Transpersonal Psychology,* October 1980, p. 29.

9. Redfering, David L., Effects of Meditative-Relaxation Exercises on Non-Attending Behaviors of Behaviorally Disturbed Children. *Journal of Clinical Psychology,* October 1979, p. 126.

10. Kratter, Jonathan and Hogan, John D., The Uses of Meditation in the Treatment of Attention Deficit Disorders with Hyperactivity. *Research in Education,* December 1983, p. 12.

11. Ferguson, Phillip C., Transcendental Meditation and Its Potential Application in the Field of Special Education. *Journal of Special Education,* Summer 1976, p. 44.

Chapter 12

1. Brown, Barbara B., *New Mind New Body.* New York: Bantam Books, Inc., 1975, p. 5.

2. Carter, John L. and Russell, Harold, Use of Biofeedback Relaxation Procedures with Learning Disabled Children, in *Stress in Childhood,* James H. Humphrey, Editor. New York: AMS Press, Inc., 1984, p. 227.

3. Houts, Arthur C., Relaxation and Thermal Feedback Treatment of Child Migraine Headache: A Case Study. *American Journal of Clinical Biofeedback,* Fall/Winter 1982, p. 154.

4. Omizo, M.M., Cubberley, W.E., Semands, S.G., and Omizo, S.A., The Effects of Biofeedback and Relaxation Training on Memory Tasks Among Hyperactive Boys. *Exceptional Children,* March 1986, p. 56.

5. Raymer, R. and Poppen, R., Behavioral Relaxation Training with Hyperactive Children. *Biofeedback and Self Regulation,* February 1984, p. 259.

6. Karnes, Frances A., Oehler, Judy J., and Jones, Gary E., The Relationship Between Electromyograph Level and the Children's Personality Questionnaire As Measures of Tensions in Upper Elementary Gifted Students. *Journal of Clinical Psychology,* March 1985, p. 164.

7. Hughes, Howard, Henry, David, and Hughes, Anita, The Effects of Frontal EMG Biofeedback Training on the Behavior of Children with Activity-Level Problems. *Biofeedback and Self-Regulation,* May 1980, p. 207.

Index

Abuse, stress of, 66-67
Achievement, of others, 37
ACTH (adrenocorticotropic hormone), 7, 8
Activities, body image
  Body Tag, 62-63
  Busy Bee, 60
  Changing Circles, 62
  Everybody Goes, 60-61
  Mirrors, 61
  Move Along, 62
Activity program, 114-115
Acute fatigue, 123-124
Adenosine, 125
Adrenalin, 7
Adrenals, 7
Affection, 55
Age
  daily hassles and, 18
  emotional needs by, 31-35
Aggression, 27-29, 37
  relaxation and, 138
Agility, 112
Aikman, Ann, 116
Alarm reaction, 8
Alimentary canal, 97, 98
Allen, Richard, 125
Amino acid, 89
Anemia, 90
Anger, 27
Animal meats, 90
Anthony, William A., 130
Anxiety, 4-5, 71
Appetite, decrease in, 101-102
Arousals/reactions, emotional, 25-30
Ash constituents, 93
Aspiration levels, 31
Assertiveness, 29

Associated Professional Sleep Societies, 129
Auditory perception, 156
Autonomy, 50-51
Auxiliary skills, 118
Avoidance behavior, and relaxation, 138-139

Balance, 113
Barbarin, Oscar A., 79
Bassin, Donna T., 86
Beckman, Paula, 80
Behavioral reaction, 10-11
Behavioral relaxation training (BRT), 160-161
Belonging, 55
Benson, Herbert, 131
Biofeedback
  with children, 159-162
  definition, 155-156
  electroencephalograph (EEG), 157-158
  electromyography (EMG), 157
  feedback thermometers, 157
  galvanic skin response (GSR), 158-159
Biofeedback training (BT), 155
Blood pressure, 9
Body control, 47
Body image, 58-60
  activities, 60-63
Body segments, 110-111
Body Tag, activity, 62-63
Body types, 109-110
Brain damage, stress-induced, 19
Brain function, and sleep, 127
Bremner, J. Douglas, 19

169

Order a copy of this book with this form or online at:
http://www.haworthpress.com/store/product.asp?sku=5210

CHILDHOOD STRESS IN CONTEMPORARY SOCIETY

_____in hardbound at $39.95 (ISBN: 0-7890-2265-6)

_____in softbound at $24.95 (ISBN: 0-7890-2266-4)

Or order online and use special offer code HEC25 in the shopping cart.

COST OF BOOKS_____

POSTAGE & HANDLING_____
(US: $4.00 for first book & $1.50
for each additional book)
(Outside US: $5.00 for first book
& $2.00 for each additional book)

SUBTOTAL_____

IN CANADA: ADD 7% GST_____

STATE TAX_____
(NY, OH, MN, CA, IIL, N, & SD residents,
add appropriate local sales tax)

FINAL TOTAL_____
(If paying in Canadian funds,
convert using the current
exchange rate, UNESCO
coupons welcome)

☐ **BILL ME LATER:** (Bill-me option is good on
US/Canada/Mexico orders only; not good to
jobbers, wholesalers, or subscription agencies.)

☐ Check here if billing address is different from
shipping address and attach purchase order and
billing address information.

Signature_____

☐ **PAYMENT ENCLOSED:** $_____

☐ **PLEASE CHARGE TO MY CREDIT CARD.**

☐ Visa ☐ MasterCard ☐ AmEx ☐ Discover
☐ Diner's Club ☐ Eurocard ☐ JCB

Account # _____

Exp. Date_____

Signature_____

Prices in US dollars and subject to change without notice.

NAME_____

INSTITUTION_____

ADDRESS_____

CITY_____

STATE/ZIP_____

COUNTRY_____ COUNTY (NY residents only)_____

TEL_____ FAX_____

E-MAIL_____

May we use your e-mail address for confirmations and other types of information? ☐ Yes ☐ No
We appreciate receiving your e-mail address and fax number. Haworth would like to e-mail or fax special
discount offers to you, as a preferred customer. **We will never share, rent, or exchange your e-mail address
or fax number.** We regard such actions as an invasion of your privacy.

Order From Your Local Bookstore or Directly From
The Haworth Press, Inc.
10 Alice Street, Binghamton, New York 13904-1580 • USA
TELEPHONE: 1-800-HAWORTH (1-800-429-6784) / Outside US/Canada: (607) 722-5857
FAX: 1-800-895-0582 / Outside US/Canada: (607) 771-0012
E-mailto: orders@haworthpress.com

For orders outside US and Canada, you may wish to order through your local
sales representative, distributor, or bookseller.
For information, see http://haworthpress.com/distributors

(Discounts are available for individual orders in US and Canada only, not booksellers/distributors.)
PLEASE PHOTOCOPY THIS FORM FOR YOUR PERSONAL USE.
http://www.HaworthPress.com   BOF04